MW00772636

"I love this book. Sherry Knowlton shares some amazing stories that a life of travel brought her way, and these were not ordinary adventures that she and her husband Mike experienced over the years. Coming from the travel industry myself, I found reading *Beyond the Sunset* both calming and exciting—a perfect escape from the times we have endured the past few years. I highly recommend it and can't wait for more. Sherry, keep traveling and sharing your stories." —**Steve Cox, a founder of International Expeditions and CEO of Conservancy Travel**

"*Beyond the Sunset* is an exhilarating read . . . The stories are interspersed with beautiful photographs from the trips too. Lush with sensory detail and brimming with diverse travel experiences, *Beyond the Sunset* is bound to appeal to seasoned and unseasoned travelers alike."
—Independent Book Review

★★★★★ "Whether recounting an unforgettable journey that took her to Woodstock for the famous music festival in the 1960s . . . or trekking through Indian forests searching for elusive tigers, she recounts adventures with a flair and talent that made me feel almost like I was a part of the journey. . . . Whether you are an armchair traveler or one who seeks more adventure, Knowlton's memoir is sure to impress."
—Manhattan Book Review

★★★★ "*Beyond the Sunset* . . . is exquisitely written by award-winning author Sherry Knowlton. She takes readers on an adventure across the world. From the national parks of the U.S. Virgin Islands to the pristine waters of the Puerto Rican coast and far beyond, Knowlton recounts the details of each destination with clarity . . . Her expertise, gift with words, and amazing photographs all contribute immensely."
—San Francisco Book Review

"Readers of Sherry Knowlton's Alexa Williams books will not be surprised to learn she's an inveterate traveler. As I read her new travel memoir, *Beyond the Sunset*, I was struck by how much Knowlton's writing reminded me of Delia Owens'. While Owens established herself as a nonfiction conservation writer before breaking into fiction, Knowlton began as a novelist and now demonstrates her formidable skills and extensive knowledge in her first travel memoir. I can hardly wait to see where Knowlton will take me next. Whether it's in fiction or non-fiction, I'm sure I'll she'll leave me engaged, entertained, and better educated about the world." —**Gerri Almand, Author of** *The Reluctant RV Wife,* *Home Is Where the RV Is,* **and** *Running from Covid in our RV Cocoon*

— **Praise for the Alexa Williams Suspense Series** —

Dead on the Delta

"Every page of *Dead on the Delta* radiates Knowlton's love and knowledge of this unique part of our planet and highlights its potential for disaster. Knowlton's suspenseful book sets the beauty of the Okavango against the dangers that lurk there." —**Michael Stanley, Author of the Detective Kubu series, also set in Botswana**

". . . a gripping new adventure for Alexa Williams. Set against the backdrop of Botswana's Okavango Delta, Alexa faces brutal poachers and a frightening conspiracy that reaches all the way to the top of Botswana's elite. The situation comes to a head in a terrifying confrontation that requires all of Alexa's strength as she fights for her own survival. A satisfying read set in a gorgeous landscape." —**Michael Niemann, award winning author of the Valentin Vermeulen thrillers**

★★★★ "full of action, adventure, politics, and, of course, animals."
—*Manhattan Book Review*

★★★★★ "great cast of characters and a fantastic female lead. Now I want to read the other books in the Alexa Williams series."
—*San Francisco Book Review*

* * *

Dead of Winter

". . . a searing tale of murder, love, and communal fear. From flying drones to police investigations and legal wrangling, *Dead of Winter* will keep you guessing and glued raptly to your reading chair." —**Gayle Lynds, *New York Times* best-selling author of *The Assassins***

". . . a riveting mystery that will stick with you long after the last page is turned. . . . While addressing xenophobia, racism, and America's complicated history, *Dead of Winter* is the novel we need and the story we want." —**J.J. Hensley, Author of *Bolt Action Remedy* and *Record Scratch***

"Knowlton examines the explosive combination of ignorance and fear that results in hate and violence." —**Matty Dalrymple, Author of the Lizzy Ballard Thrillers and the Ann Kinnear Suspense Novels and Shorts**

* * *

Dead of Spring

"A lawyer who yearns for the quiet life proves a magnet for murder"
—*Kirkus Reviews*

"A suspicious suicide of a powerful politician takes on new meaning when Alexa Williams's investigations uncover corruption at the heart of the fracking industry. Highly recommended." —**Mark Leggatt, Best-selling Author of International Thriller *Names of the Dead***

"a spellbinding yarn jerked straight from today's frightening headlines."
—**Kay Kendall, author of historical mysteries**

* * *

Dead of Summer

"Alexa Williams is a sassy, alpha-female heroine. The plot is knotty, lots of will-she or won't-she, all woven into an intense battle of wits that heats up every page. While reading, I could almost see the credits rolling for the movie." —**Steve Berry, *New York Times* and #1 International Bestselling Author**

"Fans of Sherry Knowlton's *Dead of Autumn*, will find summer to be an equally deadly season . . . a riveting, suspenseful read." —**Melissa F. Miller,** *USA TODAY* **bestselling author of legal thrillers and romantic comedic mysteries**

* * *

Dead of Autumn

"*Dead of Autumn* features a dead body harkening back to the crimes of an earlier era—there are conventions in genre writing that fans appreciate." —*Library Journal*

"I recommend this book to anyone who loves mysteries or rural Pennsylvania." —**Val Mueller, Author of** *The Faulkners Apprentice* **and** *The Corgi Capers*

BEYOND the SUNSET

a travel memoir

Volume 1: Adventures Outside My Comfort Zone

SHERRY KNOWLTON

Photography by Mike and Sherry Knowlton

Mechanicsburg, PA USA

Published by Sunbury Press, Inc.
Mechanicsburg, Pennsylvania

www.sunburypress.com

For information about special discounts for bulk purchases, please contact Sunbury Press Orders Dept. at (855) 338-8359 or orders@sunburypress.com.

To request one of our authors for speaking engagements or book signings, please contact Sunbury Press Publicity Dept. at publicity@sunburypress.com.

FIRST SUNBURY PRESS EDITION: September 2022

Set in Adobe Garamond Pro | Interior design by Crystal Devine | Cover by Lawrence Knorr | Cover photo: "Sundowner" by Mike Knowlton. Kenya. 2007 | Edited by Jennifer Cappello.

Publisher's Cataloging-in-Publication Data
Names: Knowlton, Sherry, author.
Title: Beyond the sunset, a travel memoir; volume 1 – adventures outside my comfort zone / Sherry Knowlton.
Description: First trade paperback edition. | Mechanicsburg, PA : Sunbury Press, 2022.
Summary: In a series of essays and anecdotes, this memoir tells the story of a small-town Pennsylvania girl who stretched her horizons, tested her limits, and traveled all over the globe. Augmented by stunning photos by Knowlton and her husband, *Beyond the Sunset* is a love letter to all those explorers with a nine to five job and a zest for travel.
Identifiers: ISBN 978-1-62006-916-5 (softcover).
Subjects: TRAVEL / General | TRAVEL / Essays & Travelogues | BIOGRAPHY & AUTOBIOGRAPHY / Personal Memoirs.

Product of the United States of America
0 1 1 2 3 5 8 13 21 34 55

Continue the Enlightenment!

For Mike, my companion on all of life's journeys, with love.

Other books by Sherry Knowlton

Dead on the Delta
Dead of Winter
Dead of Spring
Dead of Summer
Dead of Autumn

. . . for my purpose holds
To sail beyond the sunset, and the baths
Of all the western stars, until I die.

—Alfred, Lord Tennyson – *Ulysses*

Traveling—it leaves you speechless, then turns you into a
storyteller.

—Ibn Battuta

Contents

"The Leaves Whispered: Climb" by Sherry Knowlton. Caromb, Provence, France. 2016

1

Reading as the Spark

I BECAME A traveler because I love to read. Even as young as age five, I remember my mother remarking that I always had my "nose in a book." Of course, she and my father had fostered my love of stories because they both read to me daily, starting when I was just a newborn. Growing up in a small town in Southcentral Pennsylvania, I had one of those idyllic childhoods of the 1950s and '60s. A family of four, living in a new house on the edge of town. Freedom to play outside, roam the fields, cycle everywhere, ice skate and sled in the winter, disappear with friends for hours at a time. Still, I lived in a constricted world, shaped by my parents' finances and interests combined with the inherently insular nature of small-town living in the post-World War II era. My main glimpses of a larger universe came through magazines like *Life*, *Look*, the Sunday *Parade*, and the books I would devour one after the other.

Because my introduction to travel came largely through the written page, I often hark back to those early sources when I visit one of the places I read about as a child. Sitting with a family of San Bushmen as the chief dug in the sand for scorpions in Botswana's Makgadikgadi Pans, I couldn't help but think about the *National Geographics* that Mrs. Sleighter kept on the bookshelf of my third-grade classroom. I first saw African tribespeople dressed in animal skins in photographs on the pages of those magazines. There I was, years later, sitting next to a similar tribe as they chattered among themselves in their unique click language.

On a sailing trip through French Polynesia, our boat anchored one night in the lagoon of a small island called Huahine. Sitting on the deck, watching the stars, and listening to the wind rustle through the palms rimming the sandy shore, I felt for a moment that I'd slipped into a chapter of a novel I'd read in high school, James Michener's *Tales of the South Pacific*.

The typical sentence here might be "Who could have imagined?" that one day I'd visit the sights I'd read about. But, in fact, I did imagine. I did dream. And I credit those early imaginings and dreams with spurring my love of travel.

In my elementary school years, I read about the Bobbsey Twins' adventures in interesting locations like Eskimo Land, the Wild West, and the North Woods. Nancy Drew solved mysteries on exciting trips to Arizona's Shadow Ranch and Buenos Aires, Argentina. The Hardy Boys faced down bad guys in Caribbean Islands, Mexico, and South America.

Meanwhile, I went to school, church, and played with my friends in sleepy Chambersburg. Our family vacations each summer took us to nearby state parks, where we camped or rented a cabin for a week. My father, who'd served as a Navy Seabee in Europe during World War II, had seen the beaches of Normandy during the D-Day invasion. He'd celebrated the Allied victory in Paris on VE-Day. I now believe the war had drained him of any further desire to travel the world. Although he and my mother took several cruises in later years, the most exotic place they traveled with my brother and me was the Jersey Shore: Wildwood, then Stone Harbor.

However, I stretched my horizons through the written page. In my junior high and high school years, I read well beyond my grade level. Sometimes that meant I didn't fully comprehend the nuances of what I read. However, devouring everything I could get my hands on allowed my imagination to soar. I walked with Robert Jordan in the Pyrenees of Spain as he fought the Spanish Civil War in Hemingway's *For Whom the Bell Tolls*. Mary Stewart's romantic suspense novels, like *The Moonspinners* and *My Brother Michael*, made me long to visit the rugged islands of Greece. I read so much by Jane Austen, the Brontë sisters, Victoria Holt, and Daphne DuMaurier that I knew the English countryside like the main street of my hometown. Helen MacInnes's and Alistair MacLean's gripping spy/adventure novels took me on a tour of mysterious corners of the world from Brittany to Rome to Singapore to the Arctic. Authors as diverse as Joseph Conrad and Robert Ruark gave me a taste of Africa. I saw the South Pacific, Israel, and Italy through the eyes of James Michener, Leon Uris, and Irving Stone. And writers like John Steinbeck, William Faulkner, Jack London, and John D. MacDonald showed me places in America where life unspooled very differently from cloistered Chambersburg, PA.

Despite the intrinsic constrictions of small-town living, I had a lot of personal freedom during my childhood. Like other kids of that era, my brother and I would wander all over the neighborhood, returning home only when one of my parents rang a bell. By the time I was ten, I had standing permission to ride my bike to visit friends on the other side of town, play tennis, or make one of my frequent trips to the library. I'd be away for hours, and no one would worry. I had to adhere to curfews and geographical boundaries established by my parents, but life in placid Chambersburg was a safe zone for my friends and me to roam and explore.

Still, I knew that a broader world existed out there. I'd laze in the porch swing at my grandparents' house and watch cars whiz by on the Lincoln Highway, wondering where they might be going. One classmate's mother hailed from Germany, and another's from England. Intrigued by their accents, I'd question them about their native countries. On hot summer days, my good friend Patty and I would sit on her shady front porch, each immersed in our own book. While a passerby might have seen us as two well-behaved youngsters sitting quietly, that would have been far from the truth. Instead, I was shivering in Jack London's Yukon with the heroic dog, Buck; trembling on the Scottish moors at the cry of *The Hound of the Baskervilles*; or flying high in the sky with the Vicki Barr Flight Stewardess series. And with each new book, I'd wonder what that place on the page looked like, smelled like, and felt like in real life. My curiosity about life outside my little bubble only grew.

I can't put my finger on a specific event or point in time when I knew I wanted to travel the world. But by my teens, it had become a given. Someday, I would explore these places I'd been reading about— the Rockies, Paris, Greece, and Africa. I typed a quote from Tennyson's

Ulysses on a piece of paper and pinned it to the bulletin board in my bedroom: "For my purpose holds to sail beyond the sunset, and the baths of all the western stars, until I die." I'd look at the silver stars my father had long before painted on my bedroom ceiling and dream of far-away destinations. Tennyson's words became my touchstone.

While I threw myself into studying, school activities, boys, and all the other typical angst of a teenage girl during my high school years, those travel dreams were never far away. College took me out of Chambersburg and gave me a taste of life on my own. Uncomfortable with the other alternatives, like the University of Pennsylvania in "far-away" Philadelphia, my parents approved my eventual choice of Dickinson College. Its location, Carlisle, another small Southcentral Pennsylvania town, was slightly larger and more sophisticated than my hometown, although little more than thirty miles distant. College helped me blossom, exposed me to a wider world of thought and knowledge, and provided me with a wonderful liberal arts education with majors in English Literature and Psychology. Most importantly, my Dickinson experience helped chart the course for my later travel voyages.

I met Mike Knowlton one snowy day in February of my senior year. He joined in with a group of my friends to build a snow fort on the Dickinson campus. Soon, we were dating. By late spring, he'd moved into my apartment. Although Mike and I clicked for many reasons, I was delighted to find that he, too, had been bitten by the wanderlust bug. A Carlisle native, he'd also attended Dickinson. Before we met, he'd hitchhiked to the West Coast for a while. Then, he and a friend had flown to Puerto Rico on a lark and worked there for several months. By the time my May college graduation rolled around, we'd hatched a plan to explore the country.

We outfitted Mike's van for a camping road trip, packed up our new puppy, Poco, and hit the road in early June. What could be better? We were young and in love, with no obligations and a passion for the outdoors. The road proved a wonderful experience. Every day of that trip was an adventure. I reveled in each new sight, smell, and accent we encountered. My small universe expanded with every mile we drove. Mike and I traveled in a big loop. North to Maine and then Quebec Province. Across the northern tier of the United States, dropping into Kansas City to visit a friend, then west to Colorado.

On a budget less than bare bones, we stayed in national parks and national forest campgrounds where we could camp for as little as a buck a night. We had a general sense of our route and what territory we wanted to cover but took each day as it came. If it rained, we might stay put and drive the next day. If a place, like the Oregon beaches, caught our fancy, we'd stay an extra week. Most people were friendly, although some were put off by our long hair and hippie garb.

We had some misadventures along the way, most involving our boxer-beagle mix, Poco. As his name suggests, Poco was small, something he seemed unable to comprehend. In Provincetown on Cape Cod, he tried to play with a larger Scottie that bit his snout, leaving puncture wounds so deep they needed attention from a vet. In Quebec, Poco disappeared in a campground. That gave me a real-time lesson in the inadequacies of my high school and college French as I went from one Quebeçois camper to another, getting blank looks as I inquired about our *petit chien*. However, we found Poco in plenty of time for the pup to resume his seat on the center console for the next leg of our journey.

By the time we reached Colorado, we'd run low on cash. So, we looked for jobs. Our first choice, Boulder, didn't pan out, so we moved on to Jackson Hole, Wyoming, and found a cheap campground on the edge of town. I got a job waitressing on the night shift at a nearby diner. I waited on a steady stream of drunken cowboys who spilled out of the bars at closing time. Mike washed dishes in a bakery and took a lot of guff for his long hair from many of those same cowboys. We adopted another dog, a friendly Doberman-Labrador mix, previously owned by a fellow camper who'd been neglecting him. During our off-hours, we spent every moment exploring the Snake River and the Tetons, wading and playing in the crystal-clear water with the dogs, and hiking the many trails in the park.

A month later, we'd earned enough money to continue traveling, so, with Poco and now Zeke, we headed off to Yellowstone and then into northern Montana, taking meandering "shortcuts," which often turned out to be day-long drives on dirt roads in the middle of nowhere. We frequently had to slow down to avoid the free-range cattle that treated the sketchy roads as their territory, but traversing the open grasslands and the towering wilderness almost entirely on our own was exhilarating. I loved the adventure, that anticipation of what new animal, sight, or encounter might wait around the next bend.

As the trip continued west, I saw the Pacific Ocean for the first time. We explored the misty, mossy San Juan Islands of Washington, then headed south through Oregon and down California's spectacular Route 1. We spent a lot of time on the Oregon beaches, finding starfish and playing fetch with the dogs.

San Francisco, Big Sur, and the giant redwoods were highlights of the coastal drive. The California segment of the trip evoked so many literary and musical touchpoints that it often felt like I was revisiting territory when, in fact, I'd never seen any of it. As I admired the beautiful coastline of Monterey, I couldn't help but think about the sardine factories of Steinbeck's *Cannery Row*. Some days, Jack Kerouac was *On the Road* with us as we set out to explore Route 1. I'd interviewed the Beat Poet Allen Ginsberg for my college newspaper, so I couldn't help but think of lines from his opus *Howl* as we roamed the streets of San Francisco. In 1972, the Haight-Asbury scene was on the wane, veering from its earlier sunshine-and-flowers simplicity into something darker. However, the songs of Jefferson Airplane and countless other psychedelic bands rang in our heads as we played counterculture tourists in a quick walk-through of this legendary section of the famed city on the bay.

Near Los Angeles, we turned east, striking out for Nevada and the Grand Canyon. We stopped in Reno. Although we couldn't afford to gamble, we were dazed and slightly overwhelmed by the bright casinos and nonstop, 24/7 motion. Soon we fled the lights and glitz for nature and the northern rim of the Grand Canyon.

Disaster struck in the lonely desert after leaving the awe-inspiring national park at night. Our aging van leaked all its oil, and the engine seized. Completely dead, our home on the road had to be towed to Flagstaff, Arizona.

A few days later, after living out of the now-defunct van in a gas station parking lot, we tapped into some meager savings back home, wired to us from our parents through Western Union. We used those funds and the van as a trade-in to cobble together enough money to buy a car. When we left the garage in Flagstaff, the 1968 Javelin was packed to the brim with our camping gear and two dogs. We headed home, sleeping on picnic tables to avoid rattlesnakes in the desert night and then, after we crossed the Mississippi, in the car at rest stops. Luckily, the only rattlesnakes we saw appeared during the day when we could avoid them, and the frequent police patrols permitted us to sleep undisturbed at the rest areas.

We made few other stops on the drive home as the "bargain" muscle car burned up our dwindling funds with each gallon of gas. The places we'd wanted to visit in Texas and America's South blew by outside the window, unseen as we passed. When we reached Pennsylvania four days after leaving Flagstaff, we had thirty-eight cents between us and two dogs weary from hours jammed into a cramped car.

Some people may have been daunted by such an ignoble end to a grand adventure across America and decided never to travel again. But Mike and I loved the experience: seeing new places, meeting new people, viewing animals in the wild, staying in some of our country's most spectacular national and state parks and forests. Each wild slice of America was wonderful, but Acadia, the Grand Tetons, Yellowstone, Glacier, the beaches of Oregon and northern California, and the Grand Canyon stood out, each for its own unique natural beauty. We've returned to many of those sites often.

Our road trip brought the two of us closer together. We married that fall, and our four-month sojourn across the country became a launchpad for many more trips throughout our almost fifty years together (and counting). This book chronicles not just my journeys but my journeys with Mike and their importance to our life together. After that first exhilarating taste of the open road in our hippie van, we've never stopped traveling.

"Railroad Track" by Sherry Knowlton. Mt. Holly Springs, Pennsylvania, United States. 1974

2

The Comfort Zone

TRAVELING AS widely as Mike and I do, we've discovered that frequent travelers are a unique breed. For years, we found only a handful of friends and family who heard the siren call of the road and had any interest in joining us on trips. But on our journeys, we met others who love the lure of the unknown as much as we do. We often travel with some of those we've met along the way, people for whom travel seems intrinsic to their genetic makeup.

What makes a person susceptible to the lure of travel? Why does reading about an interesting locale make one avid reader immediately want to see it for herself, and another simply appreciate the story without any residual desire to go there? Over the years, I've come to think of the compulsion to travel as part of a broader life approach familiarly known as stepping outside the comfort zone.

Although my childhood travel was limited, from time to time, I got a taste of the world that existed outside of my daily sphere. Those brief forays into the larger world only whetted my appetite for more. My father's mother lived in Washington, DC, until my late teens. As a kid, I visited Grandma Anne and her husband, Red, a few times each year. At Thanksgiving, the entire family would go into center city and tour the lavishly decorated windows of the big department stores, often animated with scenes of spinning snowmen and elves making toys. However, I looked forward most to the summer breaks when I'd spend several weeks at her big rambling house on a hill in Southeast DC. Grandma would take off work, and we'd tour the national monuments, go to the zoo, ride the trolley, and watch Fourth of July fireworks explode over the National Mall from the panoramic vantage point of her front porch.

Often, I'd go to a vacation program at the elementary school next door to Grandma Anne's house—my chance to mingle with the city kids. Other times, my Navy brat second cousins would arrive and regale me with stories of life on the many military bases where their dad had been stationed. My fire chief step-grandfather would take me to Fort Belvoir, where he worked. And, on special occasions, my great-aunt Lesta or grown-up cousin Kay would breeze in for a visit. I loved to hear their stories of life in Taiwan and other overseas countries where they'd done stints for the State Department. To this day, I cling to the fantasy that the glamorous Kay worked for the CIA.

Grandma Anne and Red also introduced my brother and me to the joys of travel. They took us on several extended trips that gave me a tiny glimpse of life on the road. We visited the Navy family as they moved from Groton, Connecticut, to Norfolk, Virginia. We toured the forests of my home state and marveled at the steep green walls of the Pennsylvania Grand Canyon in Wellsboro. In the Great Smoky Mountains, I saw my first bear when the furry creature lumbered right up to our car window! We visited Williamsburg and learned about colonial times from people dressed in historical garb. We marveled at the water thundering over Niagara Falls from the New York side. During these trips, we stayed in motor courts, swam at their postage-stamp-sized pools, and ate at Formica-topped tables in their coffee shops. On the road, we stopped at reptile farms, pottery factories, Roadside America, and random local sights. Amazing experiences for a sheltered, small-town elementary school student.

Meanwhile, my geographic radius back home expanded just a bit too. My mother's parents bought a small summer place on the Potomac in nearby West Virginia, and we spent many weekends there on the deep river, waterskiing and eating the endless fried chicken Nanny cooked in an iron skillet the size of a tractor tire. Plus, my Girl Scout Troop took annual bus trips to places like Altoona's Horseshoe Curve, an early marvel of railroad engineering, and Virginia's Luray Caverns, which I found a little claustrophobic despite the fascinating stalactites and stalagmites.

My personal travel voyage began in earnest, however, when I saw New York City for the first time on my senior class trip in 1968. The skyscrapers and crowds of people were dazzling. An entirely different universe than the only other big cities I'd seen, Washington, DC, and, briefly, Philadelphia for a medical appointment. In my college years, I explored New York several more times with a college roommate who lived in nearby northern New Jersey. We toured museums, took in the anti-establishment rock musical *Hair* on Broadway, and spent hours hanging out in Greenwich Village trying to look cool.

I also took several trips with my friend Winnie during college breaks. My parents permitted those excursions in a sincere if somewhat reluctant attempt to acknowledge my growing independence. Winnie and I packed a tent, sleeping bags, and food and set off for a weekend on our own at the Philadelphia Folk Festival. Mingling with the crowds of strangers and drinking in the folk music scene so popular at that time, we delighted in the novelty of a weekend away from our parents.

Another time, the two of us drove to Montreal, Canada, to visit Winnie's aunt. That trip brought my first brush with the law when we were pulled over for speeding. The New York State trooper took a long look at us—two young girls driving my parents' Chrysler LeBaron—and checked the registration an interminable amount of time but finally let us off with just a warning. As to Montreal, the brief glimpse of the city's ornate stone buildings felt both new and familiar. Although I'd never seen such architecture, the buildings, gray with the patina of age and sophistication, were like those I'd envisioned when I read books set in the cities of Europe. *Les Misérables* come to life. Now I'd taken a road trip on my own and stepped outside of my home country. I knew this was just the beginning.

The summer following my freshman year of college, some friends and I purchased tickets to a weekend music concert in Bethel, New York. On the drive north from Chambersburg, we could barely contain our high spirits at seeing a concert with so many well-known bands. We looked forward to camping out for the weekend. But none of us had any idea that we were driving into history. Since my group of friends arrived well-prepared with food, tents, and other supplies, the surprising attendance of nearly 500,000 at Woodstock presented few problems for us. We arrived a day early and beat most of the traffic, then stayed an extra day for the same reason. However, the days in between proved extraordinary. I saw an iconic list of singers and bands play day and night under both clear skies and pouring rain, participated in my first yoga class at the Hog Farm, and marveled at the diverse, mostly joyous mix of humanity that had gathered for what would become a legendary "Three Days of Peace and Music."

I loved almost every minute of Woodstock, even the rain. The sheer mass of humanity dazzled me, but I was more taken by the individuals I met there. Soon after we set up our campsite, a group of musicians pulled in next to us and spilled from a panel van with their band's name embellished on the side. We got to know the members of David Peel and the Lower East Side over the next few days. Sitting around the campfire and listening to them sing, I marveled at their far-out hippie garb and carefree attitudes. When I returned home, I tracked down Peel's first album. He later became a counterculture icon in New York City and a friend of John Lennon. Lennon produced one of Peel's later albums and even mentioned the street performer by name in his song, "New York City." Of course, at Woodstock, I knew nothing about Peel and his band. I just soaked in the novel experience of hanging out with musicians who lived in NYC and had recorded an album.

Elsewhere on the sprawling farm that hosted the festival, I studied the vendors along the wooded Groovy Way who were as diverse as the goods they sold. Earth Mother-types, wholesome and maternal, invited me to experience their handmade candles or woven wares. Hippies high on life and often something more tempted shoppers with everything from hashish to patchouli oil. Wiry men with fringed vests, broad smiles, and hawklike eyes, peddled their mescaline and acid.

Sampling one of the Hog Farm's nutritious but somewhat bland meals, I talked to some of the gregarious servers and idly speculated about life in a commune. Although the group was pleasant—and their food ended up feeding many concertgoers who'd arrived without adequate provisions—I had zero interest in living a communal farming life. I'm much too introverted and averse to extended physical labor.

Of course, the music was the big constant of the weekend and could be heard wherever I wandered. One of my most vivid memories was a walk I took with Winnie to look for the boyfriend she'd arranged to meet at the concert. Sun beating on our backs, we strolled down a dirt road. As we drew parallel with the concert zone, Country Joe and the Fish broke into the "I Feel Like I'm Fixing to Die" rag. A few minutes later, a guy with the festival logo on his tee-shirt driving a concert vehicle flagged us down. He handed us each a stack of programs and asked us to distribute them as we continued the trek back to our campsite.

Another vivid memory holds a tinge of disappointment that has stayed with me for more than five decades. Weary and damp from the intermittent bouts of rain on Saturday, most of our group left the concert area around midnight and went back to the tents. I stayed with two of the guys, Mark and Dave, because we wanted to see Jefferson Airplane perform. We worked our way through the crowd, creeping closer and closer to the stage until we found a space only ten feet distant. There, we stood and watched Janis Joplin's astounding set, near enough that we could see the sweat on her brow and almost smell the frequent swigs of bourbon she took to fuel her performance. By the time Janis stopped singing around three o'clock in the morning, the headache that had been nibbling at my temple for hours had exploded into a full-blown migraine. Two more bands were slated to perform before the Airplane took the stage. Knowing those performances could take several more hours, the three of us decided to forgo hearing Grace Slick sing "White Rabbit." Looking at the daunting size of the crowd behind us on the slope, we came up with a plan to avoid the uphill slog through that mass of humanity. Instead, we snaked forward through the few rows of people in front of us and knocked at a door in the fence beneath the stage. With Mark on one side and Dave on the other holding me up, I slumped forward when a staff person opened the door.

"Hey, man," Dave said. "She's sick. We need to get her to the medical tent."

The guy took one look at my dishevelment and the pallor of my face, white from the migraine and sheer exhaustion.

"Sure. Let me get someone to lead you through," he said. "The tent is up the hill to the left."

Our subterfuge saved us considerable effort and paved the way for a quick walk back to the campsite. Even my migraine couldn't stop me from joining in the guys' laughter after we exited the stage area. I consider the harmless exaggeration of my condition my best performance in a supporting role. The Airplane didn't take the Woodstock stage until eight o'clock Sunday morning. Headache aside, it's unlikely I could have stayed awake that long. Yet, I've always regretted bailing on my opportunity to see the iconic group live. I never had another opportunity to see the band.

When I returned home, it took repeated washings to get all the mud out of my bell-bottom jeans, but I could still hear Jimi Hendrix's early morning version of "The Star-Spangled Banner" ringing in my head. Woodstock was a watershed not only in American history but in my parents' acknowledgment that I was becoming my own person with interests and independence they could no longer completely control.

By the time I'd attended Woodstock, I knew I was inclined to push the boundaries. But an incident from my childhood suggests I'd started testing the limits much earlier. On summer days, my best friend and I would often take off on our bikes and roam for hours. One afternoon, we decided to cross the river near the local college and explore an island we'd never visited. The only way to get there was to jump off our bicycles and push them across a railroad trestle.

I'll never forget the mix of sensations that day: the hot sun beating on our backs; the extra effort it took to push the bike tires over the wooden slats of the bridge; the instant of absolute terror when the tracks began to vibrate; and the exhilaration I felt as the train blew by us just moments after we'd raced to safety on the island. Looking back on that day from my eleventh summer, I realize that this experience illustrated a trait I've embraced ever since: stepping outside my comfort zone and testing my limits. Travel has been another way I've pushed the boundaries.

Today, Mike and I take trips all over the world, some well off the beaten path. Several friends call the places we visit "crazy." I call them essential. I feel the same sense of exhilaration that I felt on that hot summer day on the railroad trestle when I walk the Amazonian rainforest or wake to hear a leopard on his nighttime prowl outside our tent in the Serengeti.

I don't consider myself a thrill seeker. I don't freefall from airplanes or shoot waterfalls by kayak. Even that long-ago day on the railroad tracks, I sensed little danger. The trestle was low, and I was a good swimmer.

But for me, it's essential to try new things, meet new people, learn different customs, and see the world. I know I won't be completely happy unless, from time to time, I can feel that track vibrating.

"Spirit Bear" by Sherry Knowlton. Great Bear Rainforest, British Columbia, Canada. 2018

3

Hiking the Backcountry

URING MY twenties, hiking and camping formed the heart of my travels. Mike and I both loved the outdoors and had done considerable camping as children and teens. Plus, our hippie trip around the country had deepened our appreciation for our country's wild spaces. Equally important, hiking didn't cost a lot of money, which suited our finances, or lack thereof, perfectly. In retrospect, I realize that hiking and camping taught us a lot of lessons we've incorporated into our subsequent travels. That Scout motto "Be Prepared" should be the foundation of any hike and works just as well to undergird travels around the world. But, as we learned, fully embracing that motto often comes only with hard experience.

Our trekking days began with my husband and me spending weekends hiking the forests near our home or local sections of the Appalachian Trail. Gradually, we expanded our radius, sometimes with friends. We hiked trails in Western and Central Pennsylvania. We ventured into New England with treks in the White Mountains of New Hampshire. Then, for several years in a row, we spent a week or two each September in Maine's Acadia National Park. One fall, we headed into Canada's Maritime Provinces, going as far north as the Bay of Fundy and its world-record tide flow. The solitude and beauty of forests and mountains beckoned, and we answered the call.

The rocky crags and forests of *The Last of the Mohicans* became our stomping grounds. We saw firsthand how easily being a "swinger of birches" might entrance Robert Frost. We had frequent opportunities to experience the connection with nature that Henry David Thoreau extolled in *On Walden Pond*.

These days, I can barely remember that young woman in braids who would hoist a sleeping bag and twenty-five-pound backpack on her shoulders and hit the trail for days at a time. But I can still recall sensations like the springy give of soft pine needles under my hiking boots or the rough texture of granite under my hands as I scrambled up a rocky scree. The thrill of climbing to the top of a steep trail to take in a panoramic view garners an immediate reward for the effort that's hard to beat. Along with the total immersion in nature, hiking brings a sense of accomplishment for making it to the crest of that mountain, finishing that trek we mapped out, or dabbling our feet in that alpine stream surrounded only by birdsong and soaring peaks.

Our most ambitious hike in the Appalachians took place the day we climbed Mt. Washington. Located in New Hampshire, Mt. Washington is the highest peak in the Northeastern United States at 6,288.2 feet and has famously erratic weather. Until topped by a cyclone wind gust on Barrow Island, Australia, in 1996, Mt. Washington held the world record for directly measured surface wind speed at 231 mph.[1] Similarly, the mountain weather station has broken numerous low-temperature records, with the lowest at minus fifty degrees Fahrenheit. The automobile route to the peak is so steep and winding that the operators created bumper stickers that proclaim *I Climbed Mt. Washington*. Tourists can also take a cog railroad to the top.

But our group of three (Mike, friend and frequent hiking companion Craig Zwillinger, and me) was young, fit, and perhaps a bit overconfident. Our daypacks were stocked with water, lunch, snacks, raingear, and down jackets. We started out from Pinkham Notch at dawn, having calculated that the hike up and down would take most of the day.

What a day.

As we climbed higher, the rocky trail became almost vertical. We often stopped to rest. In mid-September, we didn't have to worry about freezing temperatures or gale-force winds. Nor did we have to deal with the draining heat of a summer day. But it was tough. Really difficult.

---

[1] Recorded on the afternoon of April 12, 1934.

One of the most challenging hikes I'd ever done. It's just over four miles to the top, but the rise is 4,300 vertical feet. The hiking guides call it strenuous, especially the headwall of the ravine and then the final push up to the summit cone.

What a shock when we reached the top though. After sweating the ascent, we had to don our down jackets on the observation deck against the chill of the freezing wind. Ice coated much of the outdoor equipment.

Inside the observatory, we came across a list of people who had died on Mt. Washington, a sobering reminder that the climb up this mountain was not only hard but could also be dangerous. At the date of this writing, the deaths on record (1849-2020) total 161 people.[2] Some of those who died were skiers or winter climbers. But many died in summer and autumn from falls, exposure during sudden bad weather, or heart attacks. Quite a number of these deaths had occurred in Tuckerman's Ravine, the route we'd taken to the top.

After a rest and lunch of peanut and butter jelly sandwiches, we took one last look at the panoramic view. Luckily, we arrived on one of those achingly clear and flawless autumn days. Since Mt. Washington is the highest point on the East Coast, we could see not only New Hampshire but Maine, Vermont, Massachusetts, New York, and even some of Canada. From that summit, it felt like we were standing on top of the world.

Tearing ourselves away from the view, we started the walk down in the early afternoon. To avoid retracing the rough trail back to Pinkham Notch, we decided to follow the autoroute. Easy, right? Our thinking went something like, "If it's set up for cars, it should be a piece of cake."

Not so much. The road was unpaved with loose gravel that rolled under our hiking boots, making for lots of unsteady steps and even slips. The serpentine path that allows cars to loop back and forth as they climb the mountain added several more miles to our journey than the morning's direct path. And there weren't even guardrails to sit on when we wanted to take a rest.

Those who've walked down steep slopes know that the constant pressure of descent can be painful on the knees. By the time we reached

---

2 New Hampshire Magazine Staff "Mt. Washington's Fatalities." Accessed November 16, 2021.
   https://www.nhmagazine.com/mount-washingtons-fatalities/

the bottom of the 7.6-mile road, my legs throbbed and I was totally exhausted. That hike stands out as the most physically demanding day I'd experienced at that point in my life. But it was exhilarating and something to treasure. To this day, Mike and I still see the occasional car with the *I Climbed Mt. Washington* sticker on its bumper. We always snort and proclaim, "So did we. But we hiked it!"

With mountains still calling us, the Appalachians soon struck us as tame. The challenge of Mt. Washington conquered, Mike and I remembered the Tetons and the other Western ranges we'd seen on our hippie road trip. Soon, our hikes centered on the Rocky Mountains. Our annual fall trips stretched to two weeks, and we backpacked in Rocky Mountain, Grand Teton, and Yellowstone National Parks.

Spending days at a time in the backcountry without encountering a human other than your companions is the best way to fully immerse yourself in nature. But backpacking also requires planning, staying alert to danger, and being prepared for the unexpected. The surprises we'd encountered on Mt. Washington taught us to plan even more carefully.

One of our longest treks was a weeklong hike into the Teton backcountry of Wyoming. Once again, Craig Z. came along. So much time has passed that I can't recall our exact route, but I do remember reaching glacier-fed mountain lakes that sparkled like jewels in the high-altitude sun and walking ridge-top trails that came so close to the Grand Teton that it felt as if we could reach out and touch the peak. However, we were hiking the high country (not doing technical climbing), so the 13,700-foot summit of that pinnacle or any of the mountain range's other peaks soared far above us.

When hiking the Rockies, bears present one of the biggest dangers. We wore bear bells intended to alert both black bears and grizzlies to our presence. For the same reason, we talked as much as we could while hiking. At night, we placed all our food into "bear-proof" bags and hoisted them high into the limbs of trees. And we carried bear spray and learned all the techniques for playing dead if attacked.

Although we've seen many bears in the wild, most have been at a distance. We've never had a run-in while hiking. During this long backpack trip in the Tetons, we did come near a grizzly in some bushes. We froze at the sounds of the snuffling animal, talked loudly to alert it to our presence, and prepared for the worst. But the animal moved away and avoided a confrontation.

A few years later, a day hiker staying at our hotel, Many Glaciers Lodge, was attacked and killed by a grizzly while we were touring Glacier National Park. Rangers closed trails and locked down the lodge area for a few days while they searched for the bear. That incident reinforced the message that grizzly danger is real. But usually, bears and other wild animals will avoid people in the backcountry. Most bear attacks on humans involve mothers with cubs or animals that have been startled. The main rule to remember with bears and other wild animals? We're guests in their world, so keep a safe distance.

The other animals we would see and hear in the backcountry were well worth the trek off the beaten path. Marmots basking in the sun. The high-pitched bugling of elk during mating season. The excited yipping of a pack of coyotes in the night. Watching a moose graze in the morning mist of a quiet pool. We've gotten quite close to mountain sheep and mountain goats, which have become somewhat habituated to humans in Glacier National Park. And hiking in Chilean Patagonia in later years, we saw a puma and llama-like guanacos.

On another of our backcountry treks, we learned that even with good preparation, we could run into trouble. This time, we were on the southwestern side of Rocky Mountain National Park in Colorado. Mike and I had planned to spend a week on the trail with my brother, Rock Rothenberger. The weather started out quite pleasant, seasonal for early September with warm days and cool nights at that altitude. But two days into the hike, a sudden, late-afternoon thunderstorm hit. The rain caught us on the side of a steep slope with little shelter, so we kept hiking to reach our assigned backcountry campsite. By the time we got to the camp spot, the temperature had dropped and we were all cold and exhausted. We started a fire immediately. Set up the tents. Changed into dry clothing. But the hour-plus of hiking in wet clothes and plunging temperatures had the three of us teetering on the edge of hypothermia.

We piled into the tent under our sleeping bags, huddled together to warm our bodies, and gradually raised our temperatures enough to reverse the danger. But we were all debilitated the next morning when we awoke. The clothes we'd worn in the storm were still heavy with moisture. Knowing we couldn't continue, we headed back to civilization. We spent the rest of the trip recuperating in a motel and touring the park from our car.

The *Sierra Club Magazine* once had a regular "What Should You Do?" feature, which examined situations in which hikers, kayakers, and other outdoors lovers get in trouble and recommends how to deal with it safely if confronted with a similar situation. The lesson from that feature and from our experience is twofold. Sometimes things happen, whether minor glitches or major disasters, that none of us can control no matter how much we prepare. However, recognizing when we're in danger and devising a plan to confront it can mean the difference between life and death. In our Rocky Mountain trail experience, we couldn't have controlled the thunderstorm or the dropping temperatures. But we recognized the signs of hypothermia and acted quickly to warm ourselves. Equally important, we determined we were no longer in adequate shape to continue the hike, so we slogged back to civilization.

These days, Mike could probably still hike the wilderness, but I'm no longer able to trek long distances due to back problems and related ailments. And both of us have lost our enthusiasm for sleeping on the ground in tiny tents. But I still hobble along on day hikes when some of our trips take us to places that can only be reached on foot.

In 2018, Mike and I sailed the Great Bear Rainforest of British Columbia on a restored tugboat, the *Maple Leaf*. We saw scores of humpback whales, orcas, seals, black bears, and grizzlies as we explored the wilderness area by boat and the rigid-hull inflatables called Zodiacs. This area is also home to the Kermode bear, a rare genetic subspecies of black bear found only in the coastal temperate forests of British Columbia. Ten to twenty percent of this species are born with creamy white coats and are called Spirit Bears.

The main goal of our trip was to glimpse a Spirit Bear. Found only on three islands in the Great Bear Rainforest, Spirit Bears are the official provincial mammal of British Columbia and revered by the First Peoples of the area. We spent one day on an island where Spirit Bears had been spotted. When we disembarked from the Zodiacs, our small group walked inland through a rainforest where the moss-covered trees dripped with moisture. We followed a narrow path that paralleled the stream. I used a hiking stick to walk the rough trail, climbing over fallen trees, avoiding slippery spots, and going up and down too many gullies to count. Without Mike's help, I might not have made it to the end of the long trek.

I assumed we'd observe the bears from a viewing platform. Not quite.

Instead, our guides brought us to a halt on the bank of the stream. This spot was where we'd wait and hope that Spirit Bears would pass by. At bear level!

I was perched on a fallen tree in the creek bed when the Spirit Bear came meandering down the stream. Our guides had told us to sit still and not panic if a bear approached. Easier said than done when a several hundred-pound bear stops twenty feet away and looks you in the eye. But there she was. Huge. More a champagne color than white. But beautiful.

So, I sat there in a mixture of awe and terror, snapping photos and hoping the bear didn't decide to investigate this woman with the camera. But she seemed more interested in fishing for salmon than bothering with me. Soon, the bear ambled away, and my heart rate returned to normal.

Being that close to a wild bear, one I'd traveled hundreds of miles to see, was a magical experience. The joy of seeing a Spirit Bear in the wild outweighed the fear. When she left, I had tears of wonder in my eyes. That Spirit Bear encounter is a shining example of the rewards of a difficult hike, one I can revisit from time to time in my photos and in my memory.

In our early days of hiking, as we took precautions to avoid bears, Mike and I never imagined that, one day, we would travel thousands of miles to seek a glimpse of a bear in the wild. Although the encounter with the Spirit Bear in British Columbia had my heart racing, we knew that the bears had become habituated to the frequent adventure tourists on their island. With experienced naturalists to guide us on that bear encounter, we had minimized the risks. And minimizing risks lies at the heart of practicing preparedness. Like many young people, Mike and I had to learn some hard lessons to fully grasp how important that concept of "Be Prepared" can be. Extending ourselves physically almost to the point of exhaustion could have ended badly on Mt. Washington. If we hadn't dealt with the incipient hypothermia on that hike in the Colorado Rockies, the most extreme result could have been death. But, with each mistake, we learned how to face the wilderness better prepared. To reduce the potential for risks as well as to have the supplies and skills to face unexpected dangers. Doing so allowed us to enjoy hours of hiking, camping, and wildlife viewing in some of the most spectacular spots on earth. In fact, embracing the motto "Be Prepared" has become foundational to our broader travel adventures and everyday life.

4

Trains, Planes, and Tuk tuks

HELICOPTERS CAN provide an amazing perspective on a natural wonder. Because I have a fear of heights, I thought a helicopter flight would terrify me. I couldn't have been more mistaken. One of the most spectacular experiences I've ever had is a helicopter flight to Aoraki (Mt. Cook), the tallest mountain in New Zealand. The pilot flew us over miles of snow-covered mountain ranges before touching down on Mt. Cook. If you've seen the Beacons of Gondor being lit in the movie *The Lord of the Rings: The Return of the King*, you've glimpsed the territory we covered by air. Standing on the hard-packed snow with Mike and our son, Josh, it felt like we'd stepped into an icy fantasy world. The rest of the South Island's Southern Alps stretched out around us, literally, as far as the eye could see.

That helicopter flight was an awe-inspiring experience. However, I'm no modern-day Jay Gatsby or Bobby Axelrod (from the Showtime series *Billions*), so helicopters aren't my usual mode of transportation, even when traveling. But Mike and I have been introduced to a wide range of other transport options around the world.

One of my favorite city memories is the day Mike and I spent roaming the streets of Paris, from our hotel to Notre Dame, L'Orangerie, and the Eiffel Tower with periodic stops to simply sit at cafes and watch everyone else drift by. On that day, I pictured Ernest Hemingway, F. Scott Fitzgerald, Gertrude Stein, T. S. Eliot, Ezra Pound, and other literary expatriates of the Lost Generation doing the very same thing back

"The Delhi-Mumbai Line" by Sherry Knowlton. Ranthambore, Rajasthan, India. 2017

in the 1920s. On a similar memorable day in Venice, we wandered off the tourist trail and ambled through residential neighborhoods, crossing canals and watching the dwindling number of locals living their lives in this haunted, drowning city. Walking is essential for exploring museums, gardens, city streets, and tiny hill-towns. Likewise, immersing ourselves in nature can often best be done on foot.

However, experiencing local methods of transportation is another way to appreciate a new place. And other types of transportation become necessary to cover multiple sites during a trip or to reach far-away places.

The workhorses of long-distance travel are planes, trains, and automobiles. A fourth key option is a boat, which I'll talk more about in the following chapter. So many more variations exist for in-country travel. I find it fascinating how different regions and countries have evolved in their approaches to getting people from point A to point B.

We fly to overseas destinations and most places in the United States and Canada that are more than a few hours' drive. Our longest flight ever, to New Zealand, took almost two days from Dulles, with stops in Los Angeles and Tahiti before landing in Auckland. Our longest nonstop flight, a Singapore Airlines flight from Newark to Singapore, took eighteen straight hours on the plane. Luckily, the plane was entirely business class, so it was comfortable. During all that time in the air, I discovered one of my now-favorite drinks, Singapore Breakfast Tea, a great blend of exotic spices with a tantalizing hint of anise. But that was a long, long flight. Even wilder, Singapore was just a stop on the way to our ultimate destination, Bali.

These days, it seems that air travel inherently involves delays, cancellations, missed connections, and other hiccups. We've had so many of these it's hard to remember them all. And the increased security since 9/11 has only added extra steps and hassle to the pre-boarding process. More recently, COVID-19 protocols have presented another layer of hurdles. Although many flyers complain about the US security process, it pales in comparison to some of the more hands-on approaches in countries like India. There, men and women are screened separately and patted down thoroughly by same-gender personnel. We've had bags screened multiple times prior to boarding in airports from Schiphol to Delhi to

Bequia. During one of the worst Ebola crises in Africa, we underwent temperature checks and health screenings at airports in South Africa and Botswana, even though the Ebola outbreak was thousands of miles away in West Africa.

We had an early experience with travel during the COVID-19 pandemic, flying home from the Virgin Islands just days before quarantine brought international and most domestic travel to a screeching halt. When both Mike and I came down with a respiratory illness the next week, we thought we'd contracted the fearsome disease in the huge, milling crowds in the St. Thomas airport. However, we recovered. Subsequent testing indicated that whatever our illness was, it wasn't coronavirus. In the following year and a half, the pandemic forced us to cancel several planned trips, including one overseas.

In late summer 2021, Mike and I (fully vaccinated) took a long-delayed trip to Ireland and then flew onto Iceland. Both countries had recently opened their borders to American travelers. The trip turned out fine, but ongoing pandemic requirements for border entry, masking, COVID testing, restrictions on restaurant dining, and more definitely made things complicated and stressful.

As I write this, COVID restrictions on travel continue to change as the pandemic waxes and wanes within each country. It remains unclear when travel will fully resume around the globe. But it's likely that precautions like vaccine and testing requirements, masks, and other COVID-related measures may be with us for some time.

I'm somewhat sanguine about airport screening and other rules. I'd rather spend a few more minutes in line, having my bags searched or temperature taken, get a pre-flight COVID test, or wear a mask than die in an explosion or catch a deadly disease. It's a reasonable part of the bargain when you want to fly to the other side of the planet since air is the quickest and most efficient way to travel long distances.

I've flown so much for both business and pleasure since my first flight to the US Virgin Islands in my twenties that I have no real fear of flying. In fact, I particularly enjoy the light aircraft that are often one of the few ways to reach remote destinations—despite reading many books, like Clive Cussler's *Sahara*, that feature small plane crashes.

On a trip to see the brown and black bears at Alaska's Redoubt Bay Lodge in the Lake Clark National Park and Preserve, we flew from Anchorage to the lake in a floatplane. The pilot stashed our luggage in the pontoons before our low flight over acres of pristine Alaskan wilderness. The new experience of a water landing on Lake Clark was smooth and so much fun.

A similar, exhilarating experience was the commercial flight on regional SVG Air that flew us to and from the small island of Bequia in the multi-island nation of St. Vincent and the Grenadines. The four-seater flew so low on its way to St. Lucia that we could see small boats bobbing on the Caribbean. And many years ago, before the British Virgin Islands became a mainstream tourist destination, I remember chickens scattering on the dirt runway of Virgin Gorda when our island-hopper landed for a customs check.

Our most extensive experience with small planes, however, comes from Africa. In Botswana, Zambia, Zimbabwe, and Kenya, small planes are one of the most common ways to move between safari camps. Mike and I have twice flown on tiny planes with just us and a pilot. Other times, the planes have carried four to fourteen plus the pilot. Although we've had a few bumpy rides, the flights give passengers a panoramic view of the plains, desert, or delta below. Often, we've seen larger animals like elephants, buffalo, and giraffes. In fact, prior to landing, the pilots either buzz the runway or contact guides on the ground to clear wild animals, such as lions or zebras, that might be hanging out on the dirt landing strips. To be safe, I always stash ginger candy or Tums in my pocket—just in case we hit crosswinds or other turbulence in these light aircraft.

Aside from relying on air transportation for reaching a destination, the best way to truly appreciate a particular landmark often can be from the air. We took a small plane flight to view Mt. Everest in Nepal, a fly-by of the magnificent tallest peak in the world. When we did a flight tour of Mt. Denali in Alaska, we'd hoped that we could land on the mountain. However, the snow was too soft even for a plane with landing skis. So—still impressive—we viewed the peak and the surrounding mountain range from the air. Both tours provided us with a unique perspective on these towering peaks and the expansive mountain ranges in which they sit.

My only other helicopter experience to date, a sightseeing flight over Victoria Falls, offered a different kind of thrill. The mighty falls split the border between Zimbabwe and Zambia. Called *Mosi-oa-Tunya*, "The Smoke That Thunders," by local tribes, the natural wonder is one of the largest waterfalls in the world at its peak water flow. The helicopter ride through part of the river gorge ended with a dizzying pass over the towering drop of rushing water into the narrow chasm of the river below—a panoramic view of the falls impossible to fully see from any place on the ground.

A more serene way to take in a striking aerial view is from a hot air balloon. Twice we've taken hot air balloon rides in Africa. Once over Tanzania's Serengeti Plain. The other time over the adjoining Masa Mara plain in Kenya. The experience both thrills and calms. We left the ground just as darkness gave way to dawn. On these African balloons, we climbed into the basket as it rested on its side, sat on a seat, and clung to a strap. When the balloon heated enough for takeoff, the basket righted itself as we ascended into the sky. The pilot controls the rate of ascent, descent, and direction of the flight.

From the balloon, we had an expansive view of the wild animals below. On our Serengeti flight, one of the highlights was a mama hippo with her newborn baby. Our balloon ride over the Masa Mara coincided with the annual migration of wildebeest and zebra, and the wildebeest were calving. Even hundreds of feet in the air, we could hear the seemingly endless herds bleating and watch packs of hyena stalk the newborn calves in growing daylight. After we landed, we had an elegant champagne breakfast in the bush. What a surreal feeling to sit at a long table, complete with a starched white tablecloth and china, dining on eggs, bacon, and croissants while watching elephants stroll by in the distance.

Our balloon ride over the temple city of Bagan in Myanmar (Burma) had a much different feel. This ancient city's thousands of Buddhist temples sprawl over a flat plain near the Irrawaddy River. Once again, we took off at dawn, this time in an upright basket, and floated over a magical landscape of golden temple domes and burnished sienna spires, bathed in a rosy glow from the rising sun. Very mystical and serene.

Trains are another popular method of transportation, although the degree of efficiency can vary depending on location. Europe is a wonderful place to travel by train. The trains connect directly with many destinations and travel close to most others. Although I find watching the scenery whizzing by a bit disorienting, high-speed trains in Spain and France travel long distances in only a few hours. Another plus: train travel in Europe is inexpensive. I must note that deciphering the tickets and boarding the right train can be a bit confusing. Once, we boarded the wrong Naples-to-Rome train. The conductor didn't discover our error until the correct train had left the station. Lucky there were two Naples-to-Rome trains, and we hadn't blundered onto a track headed to another destination. After a small kerfuffle, however, the conductor found us two empty seats, and we arrived in Rome only slightly behind schedule with plenty of time to fly back home the next day.

India's trains are also workhorses but more utilitarian and timeworn. On our first time in Mumbai's train station, we stood on the elevated platform, waiting for our train to arrive, and watched waves of rats race up and down the sunken trackbed. I was elated to find that the train car itself was vermin-free and the ride bumpy but uneventful.

On another trip in India, we rode the train from Ranthambhore to Delhi. Our party of four had a private compartment with comfortable, if not luxurious, seats and a bathroom. However, the other cars on our train, like previous ones that had passed through the station, carried a swarm of humanity. People hanging off the rear platform and people sitting on the roof with standing room only inside several cars. Many people gave up and jumped off before the train picked up speed. I can't imagine how dangerous riding on the roof must be. Our ride to Delhi was a bit rough, but we reached our destination on schedule and had a chance to view miles of India as we passed by.

I traveled Amtrak to Philadelphia and New York regularly during my working years and on personal trips. But the United States lags well behind much of the world in passenger train infrastructure. So, it's notable that our northernmost state, Alaska, relies on a train to ferry thousands of visitors from Anchorage to Mt. Denali National Park every day. After driving the Kenai Peninsula to Homer on our own by rental car, Mike and I took the Alaska Railroad's Denali Star train roundtrip from Anchorage to Denali. The train serves meals and is designed for wilderness and wildlife viewing with huge dome windows that extend to the peak of the ceiling. It's like riding in a giant glass bubble. We also spent time on the outdoor viewing platforms at the back of the train car, watching the remote villages, forests, and mountain peaks flow by.

We took a similar dome-window train, the Rocky Mountaineer, on a two-week loop through the Canadian Rockies. This relaxing trip was quite deluxe, especially the food and service. Feasting on gourmet breakfasts and lunches, we wound our way through towering mountains. Through the glass bubble of our comfortable second-floor observation car, we spied bears, eagles, and mountain sheep. Mike even saw a wolf vanish into the woods as we passed. At one point, we traveled so near a mountain stream that we could see spawning salmon choking its crystal waters.

Each night, the Rocky Mountaineer stopped in a town where we were ferried to hotels. Midway through the trip, we left the train and traveled by bus to spend several days at a series of grand hotels. The Canadian Rockies are known for the huge hotels in Jasper, Banff, and Lake Louise. From the outside, these behemoths remind me of the hotel in Stephen King's *The Shining*. On the inside, they're quite pleasant, with an ambiance that hovers somewhere between historic grandeur and well-worn comfort, depending upon the lodge.

We also took a train, the Hiram Bingham, to Machu Picchu in Peru on a several-hour climb from the town of Poroy near Cusco to Aguas Calientes at the foot of the famous Incan ruins. That ride on the restored classic train included local entertainment, food, and drink, but the highlight of the trip lay outside our windows: the fields, ravines, and tall Andean peaks. We even encountered a wildfire in one of the valleys. Train staff told us that the fire was likely caused by a farmer burning off his field, a traditional agrarian practice we've seen in many places in the world. This fire had jumped the farmer's field and was now burning out of control, running up hills and down into valleys unchecked. After stopping the train to assess the situation, the engineer decided to go forward through the dense smoke. We could see flames leaping from the steep hillside only a few yards outside our windows as we chugged by. After several tense minutes, we made it through the danger and emerged without damage.

We've traveled in a wide range of motorized vehicles from cars to vans to buses, large and small. Mike and I started our travels together by circuiting the country for months in a beat-up Chevy van. These days, Mike usually drives one of our own vehicles on trips around the US. And he always takes the wheel as the primary driver when we travel together in rental cars, especially if we're in a country that drives on the left. He's navigated the steep, donkey- and chicken-filled roads of many a Caribbean island. He's steered us through rural roads and narrow village lanes in Italy and France. He drove the roads of both the North and South Islands of New Zealand for a month without incident.

My experience with foreign driving is, by choice, more limited. One of the few times I drove in New Zealand was after a dinner in Dunedin. Because both my husband and son had a beer with their meals, I became the designated driver back to our hotel. I was so tentative pulling out of the parking spot in front of the restaurant that a cop stopped me after I'd driven less than a block. He let me go with just a warning after he realized I wasn't drunk but simply terrified of driving on the left. However, when we spent five weeks on St. John in the USVI, I had to break down and drive from time to time. I must admit I hugged the center whenever the road edged by steep drop-offs (and the oncoming lane was clear).

Speaking of steep drop-offs, even Mike decided that our first drive on Italy's scenic but precipitous Amalfi Coast should be by private car with an experienced driver. The narrow, winding road is clogged with huge buses and bursting with heart-stopping views—vistas he wanted to enjoy without worrying about driving off the sheer cliffs and plunging into the sea below.

One of my favorite modes of wheeled transportation is safari vehicles, perhaps because I love safaris so much. We've spent time in several

'Elephant Escapade.' Mike and Sherry Knowlton and elephants at the …

...Four Seasons Tented Camp Golden Triangle, near Chiang Rai, Thailand. 2014

types of these vehicles, which are designed for the rugged roads of Africa's national parks and unobstructed animal viewing. In our East African (Kenya, Tanzania, Uganda) safaris, the vehicles have been enclosed for the most part, with wide windows that open. I've been close enough to passing lions that I could have reached through the window to pat them on the back—how exciting to have that proximity to a wild animal! Of course, touching one could result in a lost arm and so is not advisable.

Some of the East African vehicles have tops that pop up several feet above roof level so passengers can stand and look out at the animals. On others, the tops retract entirely, so the roof opens to the sky. We rode in the open-roof version on a particularly memorable day when we traveled to a remote area of the Serengeti Plain on the lookout for a pride of lions. Mike and I stood on the back seat, head and shoulders above the roofline, as we drove slowly for more than an hour without passing another vehicle or human, adrift on an endless expanse of rippling yellow grass and bright blue sky. We found the lion pride, and even after all these years, it's the drive I remember most. That feeling of being at the end of the earth on a glorious day that could happily have gone on forever.

My favorite safari vehicles, however, are the models more commonly used in the southern African countries of Botswana, Zambia, and Zimbabwe. The big Toyota Land Cruisers or Land Rovers, outfitted specifically for safaris, have tiered seats that allow all the passengers a clear view of the animals. These vehicles have no windows and are usually roofed with canvas that snaps off entirely if the day is not too hot. They convey the feeling that there's no barrier between passengers and the animals they see . . . because there is no barrier! And, on safari, one often can come very close to animals habituated from birth to the presence of the big vehicles.

My most heart-stopping experience in a safari vehicle came at Chitabe Camp in Botswana while tracking a leopard. We had followed her from the edge of the water into a bushy area. The guide gave her some distance until she climbed onto a small scrubby tree that barely held the big cat's weight. He pulled near the tree so we could watch the leopard as she tried to find a comfortable resting place in the swaying branches. Then, abruptly, the cat turned and started back down the tree. My seat in the vehicle was parallel to the slender trunk. I sat no more than six feet away from the leopard as she made her way down, step by step, until her head was level with my eyes. I held my breath. If she'd wanted to, the leopard could have leapt into my lap without hesitation. But her glance barely met mine as she hopped onto the ground and continued her prowl. A memorable experience made more memorable by the lack of any barrier between the cat and me.

Amalfi wasn't the only place we've booked with drivers, buses, or minibuses. Instead of navigating unfamiliar road signs in unfamiliar languages (and even strange-to-us alphabets), we've found organized tours that include transport are often the best way to get the lay of the land.

One of my first bus trips outside the country was in Spain with my son's Spanish class. The trip organizers had run similar excursions and knew the advantages of corralling high school kids into a large bus. Traveling for a week as a chaperone to thirty teenagers was an experience I will never forget, but Josh and I still reminisce about the trip, the kids' hijinks, and the beauty of Toledo, Madrid, and Seville.

Of course, the flip side of having someone else drive the bus, large or small, is that you must put your life in their hands. On our first trip to India, we found the traffic to be jaw-dropping. Imagine anywhere from five to ten rows of colorful trucks adorned with tassels and decorative painting; buses piled high with suitcases and sacks of grain; cars; motorcycles often carrying entire families, furniture, or pigs for market; tuk tuks; and wooden carts pulled by camels—all surging forward without any marked lanes. All the drivers leaning on their horns and vying for the quickest path through the morass of wheeled vehicles. Throw in a few cows—sacred to Hindus and, thus, free to wander wherever they choose, including into traffic—and you have mind-boggling chaos.

A mid-size tourist bus driven by an experienced Indian with an assistant to navigate what were, to them, familiar traffic patterns was ideal in this situation.

The most hair-raising moment on the Indian bus unfolded the day our driver needed to reach a restaurant on the other side of the divided road we'd been traveling. At a gap in the concrete barrier, he simply cut to the other side of the road and drove against oncoming traffic for about a half-mile. Several of our traveling companions, many of them elderly, began screaming. One terrified woman broke down in tears. Our guide tried to calm the group, telling us that the driver had done this many times, that he knew what he was doing. But several people kept asking the guide to repeat what he was saying. Perhaps his accent and speech rhythms were a little difficult for some to navigate in a stressful situation. Perhaps they couldn't hear over their companions' screams. At one point, Mike and I jumped in and "translated" what we thought was the guide's perfectly understandable English for our fellow passengers. In retrospect, the entire scene played out like a cheap *Airplane* knock-off that could've been called *Wrong-way Bus*.

Meanwhile, the oncoming traffic adjusted and streamed by smoothly on either side of the bus, like water flowing past a rock. When the driver turned into our destination, both the bus and its passengers had survived unscathed. However, I did notice that a few passengers walked with an unsteady gait as they made their way into the restaurant.

Two of the most interesting methods of travel, commonplace in Asia and India, are bicycle rickshaws and that strange motorized vehicle called a tuk tuk. I'd seen pedicabs in New York City, so the concept of small, pedaled taxis wasn't entirely new to me. But the first time I climbed onto the seat of a bicycle rickshaw propelled by a short, wiry Vietnamese man, I felt instant guilt. I'm not a small woman. Add a second person (Mike is quite fit but tall), and we totaled more weight than it seemed possible for our slight driver to manage. That day and every time since whenever we've used a bicycle rickshaw, we've over-tipped out of size guilt. I'm not sure Western bodies are designed to be passengers in bicycle rickshaws. They are, however, a great way to see a city at street level. Although, when the rickshaw must compete with motorized traffic, it can also be a bit scary.

In my mind, tuk tuks are marginally safer, perhaps an illusion created by whisper-thin metal walls. But they are motorized, often built in a tricycle-like configuration with a single wheel up front and two beneath the passenger compartment. Some fit two passengers. Some fit four or more. Most are partially enclosed. Others are more open. Either way, passengers get a good view of the cityscape or rural scenery as well as the pavement whirring by inches beneath their feet.

We've used tuk tuks for short trips that took forever, maybe because they seem to be more prevalent in cities with large populations and traffic-clogged streets. One tuk tuk we booked in Old Delhi became trapped so long in traffic that we got the chance to engage in extended chats with several groups of people in nearby tuk tuks. Most were so close we could have reached out to shake hands. A family with two young girls, all dressed as if for a special occasion, seemed particularly interested in our group of four Americans stuck alongside them in the sea of vehicles. They asked question after question about not only our tour itinerary but about our personal histories.

On another trip, our guide bustled our small group into tuk tuks for a long ride on a very bumpy road to a remote temple in Myanmar. That was the day we found out that tuk tuks have very poor, perhaps nonexistent, suspension systems. I felt the aches from each bone-shaking pothole and rut for days afterward.

One step down in modernization but one step up in charm are horse-drawn carriages or carts. I have twice prevailed on my husband and son to do a horse and carriage ride. Once through Old City Philadelphia, which, because of the traffic and heat, fell a bit short of the romantic ride into history I'd envisioned. But I loved the carriage ride we took early one evening through the main city on the island of Spetses, Greece. The slow pace of the carriage gave us a chance to really take in the old buildings and the people passing by. However, the charm of the horse-drawn carriages is lost on my husband. So, I was surprised when our friend Betty and I persuaded Mike to take a subsequent carriage ride through the streets of Dublin. The witty patter of the old gentleman driving the carriage more than compensated for the heavy vehicle traffic around us. Mike actually enjoyed this one.

There can be some drawbacks to relying on horses for transportation. On a sailing excursion through part of the Indonesian archipelago, we landed at Bima on Sumbawa Island and took horse carts from the dock to the center of town. A single horse pulled each of our group's bright blue wooden carts. Four of us sat in each cart upon benches facing each other, knees touching. A little bumpy but fun and a good way to people-watch, the ride into the city passed without incident. However, when we prepared to board carts for the return trip, two of the horses had a disagreement. Despite the traces that harnessed the animals to the empty wagons, they reared in the air, neighing and biting each other's necks. Horse fight! It took a while for the drivers to calm the angry animals so customers could safely clamber into waiting carts. The two warrior steeds were taken out of rotation, and we climbed into carts with more placid horses for the ride back to the harbor.

I'll confess that I'm a bit frightened of horses. My only real experience with them as a child was a brief ride on a huge, Clydesdale-sized working horse on my great-uncle Roy's farm when I was about six. My grandmother took a photo of me perched high on the horse's back, looking like I was about to burst into tears. So, it's not entirely clear why, two decades later, with no further experience on horseback, I thought a trail ride in the Rocky Mountains would be fun when Mike, a longtime equestrian, suggested it. Sometimes I go for the romantic-sounding activity without really thinking it through. *The Man Who Loved Cat Dancing* by Marilyn Durham, Zane Gray novels, and a montage of old Western movies passing through my mind overshadowed the basic fact: I'd never really ridden a horse before. Sure, why not mount up for a trail ride into the wilderness?

Most of the trail ride wasn't bad. The wranglers positioned me in the middle of a line of horses and riders that followed the guide up a well-worn path into the mountains. These horses had made this trek so many times they could have done it blindfolded. But the ride back got tricky. As we entered a broad meadow about a mile from the stables, my horse realized two things: he was hungry, and this greenhorn on his back had absolutely no idea how to control him. So, he bolted. Okay, broke into a brisk canter. Although I tried every technique I'd learned in our five-minute pre-ride briefing to stop him, I quickly gave up and just held on for dear life. We managed to arrive at the stables with me still clinging to this devil's back, but I've never been on a horse again. That old saw about climbing back on the horse that threw you? Let's just say I wasn't anxious to take the chance that the next one actually would succeed in bucking me off onto the ground.

Strangely enough, that fear of horses hasn't kept me from riding oh-so-much-larger elephants. Let me preface my elephant experiences by acknowledging that the practice of tourists riding elephants has fallen out of favor, largely because of historically abusive training and living conditions for many of the animals used for both tourism and work, such as logging. Because of the recent efforts to bring this issue to light, it's unlikely I would ride an elephant again. In both India and parts of Southeast Asia, elephants are still used for some types of commercial labor, but riding opportunities have been phased out of much of the tourist industry because of the shift in public opinion.

Some of the criticism of using elephants for transportation comes from the timeworn methods used to train and control the animals. The rider, called a *mahout*, sits right behind the elephant's head and steers the beast with his feet on the elephant's ears. We've seen mahouts use a steel stick with a hook, called a bullhook or ankus, to guide a recalcitrant elephant. Some elephants even develop a small hole in their ear from the repeated use of the hook. However, we never saw a mahout use the ankus in anger. Only once did we see harsh mistreatment of one of these powerful beasts, which was being used as a street performer in Myanmar, much like trained elephants in the now-disappearing Western circus acts.

Still, I must admit, some of my best travel experiences have been on the back of an elephant. Our first ride took place in India, where we stepped from a platform into a basket on the back of a brightly painted and adorned elephant that took us up a hill to the Amber Fort in Jaipur. I was entranced by the experience. It felt like I was living a scene from *Passage to India* or *The Far Pavilions*. In retrospect, I can appreciate what a hard, monotonous life it must be for these magnificent creatures to plod up and down a hill all day with basket-loads of tourists on their backs.

But the real thrill of riding an elephant came later that trip in Bandhavgarh National Park. We had come to see tigers in the wild, but often tigers burrow into the thick underbrush. Each day, mahouts would ride their elephants into the jungle to locate spots where tigers were resting.

Then, the mahouts would radio our guides to meet them on a road near-by. Once, we hoisted ourselves into the elephant basket from the roll bar of our open jeep. Another time, we climbed a wooden ladder propped against the elephant's side. When we settled securely in the basket, the elephant took us into the jungle to see the tigers. The big cats were so accustomed to the lumbering beasts that they didn't flee. Riding ten feet in the air, rocking back and forth as the elephants plodded through the thick jungle, felt like cruising on an ocean of green.

In Laos, we spent a few days in a very remote rural village. Staying there gave us a glimpse into a very different world. The rustic hotel. The herds of water buffalo grazing the lush wetland grass outside our porch. The Spirit Houses for offerings to the gods and the sometimes-malicious Djinn. The ramshackle houses and streets filled with exuberant children. But the best part of that stay was the ride, once again on elephant-back, to the ruins of an ancient mountain temple at dawn. The ride through the morning mist verged upon mystical. And, upon our return, we dismounted and fed our eager elephants stalks of sugar cane by hand.

My absolute best elephant interaction came in Thailand's Northern Triangle, the region where Thailand, Myanmar, and Laos meet in the middle of the Mekong River. The area is well-known as the one-time heart of the international opium trade. Perhaps it still is, but the fascinating International Opium Museum there professes that the trade is mostly a thing of the past. Mike and I stayed at the Four Seasons Tented Camp, one of those places that I saw pictured once in a magazine and wouldn't rest until we visited. Our elevated tent overlooked the Ruak River with Myanmar on the far bank.

The Four Seasons camp is home to a group of elephants rescued from abusive conditions or retired and ready for a slower life. Some of the camp's adopted elephants spend the rest of their lives cared for in the fields and the jungles on the property. Others interact with guests on a limited basis. Each morning, a few young elephants joined us at break-fast. Feeding the youngsters kept us laughing as they reached out with their trunks to snatch bananas from our hands as fast as we could pluck them from a basket.

But the clear highlight of the stay was our four-hour lesson on how to become a mahout. Dressed in denim coveralls, Mike and I joined a French couple in first learning the Thai commands for guiding an elephant. Then, we progressed to practicing several ways to mount a kneeling elephant from the ground (including scrambling up its trunk). The next phase of our instruction turned out to be a blast. Straddling the elephant's neck, we became mahouts-in-training, using our feet and the Thai commands to guide the elephant through an hour-long trek around the jungle. Even though I rode the smallest of the four elephants, I found it a little frightening to perch high above the ground on a moving animal with nothing to keep me up there other than my legs and hands. But my elephant, Phuang Pet, was a gentle and patient old dame, and I soon adjusted to the rhythm of her plodding gait. Mike rode a huge elephant; her back stood at least eleven feet off the ground. Yuki had been a TV star in Japan before the Four Seasons rescued her. But Mike quickly adapted to the big beast, also quite gentle.

Full disclosure: Each elephant's actual mahout walked alongside us during our outing. Near the end of the morning, the mahouts slipped onto the elephants behind us as they directed their charges into the muddy waters of the river. The biggest surprise came when Mike's mahout leaned forward to give his elephant a command. Seconds later, the elephant filled her trunk with water and sprayed me. Mike nearly fell off his elephant laughing. Soaking wet, I broke into peals of laughter.

That ride on the elephant brought me sheer, unadulterated joy. I may have been in my early sixties, but I felt like an eight-year-old again. The Four Seasons is doing wonderful work both in elephant rescue and bringing delight to their guests in arranging this chance for in-depth elephant-human interaction. Hands down, the best "transportation" experience I've ever had.

'Wilderness Zen' by Sherry Knowlton. Mike Knowlton near Qorokwe Camp, Okavango Delta, Botswana. 2019

Boats

I LOVE SPENDING time in a boat. Whether a way to get from one destination to another or just for pleasure, few things exist in life better than time spent on the water. Many wonderful hours of my childhood unspooled at my maternal grandparents' place on the Potomac River waterskiing and puttering around in their motorboat. I learned to canoe at Girl Scout Camp. And, later, Mike and I spent many lazy summer afternoons tubing and rafting on the Conodoquinet Creek or canoeing on one of the lakes near our home.

As we began to travel, we were introduced to new ways to get out on the water. A ferry to Washington's San Juan Islands. A float trip down Wyoming's Snake River. A short schooner cruise off the coast of Maine. Day sails from Caribbean Islands like St. Thomas, St. Martin, and St. Lucia. Those water experiences led us to sailing but also spurred us to incorporate boat trips into our journeys. Sometimes, the boat became the journey itself.

One of our first expeditions by boat came on the Amazon River in Peru. A fascinating nonfiction book, *River of Doubt*, recounts Teddy Roosevelt's harrowing journey into the Amazon rainforest. Although we had some trepidation, Amazon travel has improved dramatically in the century-plus since Roosevelt's dangerous adventure. Our boat, *La Amatista*, held twenty passengers and almost as many crew on a voyage that left the city of Iquitos and headed upstream. We traveled first on the majestic Amazon itself and then into the smaller rivers of the Ucayali River Basin. Several times, we stopped to visit villages perched on the banks of the river where we met the hardy Ribereño people who live by subsistence farming and fishing.

Each day, we would climb into smaller boats and explore small tributaries, fishing for piranhas or hiking the rainforest. The piranhas we caught became part of our evening meal. Mostly bone and teeth, these small ferocious fish were more snack than main course. But after a childhood watching jungle movies incomplete without a ferocious piranha scene, reeling in these sharp-toothed legends on a fishing rod and eating them certainly gave me bragging rights.

I loved to sit on the upper (third) deck of the boat and watch the jungles, fields, and villages as we drifted by. Although a different continent, I couldn't help but think of Marley going up an African river to find Colonel Kurtz in *Heart of Darkness* even as I found not horror but peace. Time slowed as each day we drifted farther and farther from civilization. The busy commercial traffic on the wide Amazon gave way to smaller boats, often filled with families who spend their whole lives on the water. As we steered into smaller tributaries, the channels narrowed. We saw birds, the huge-yet-cute South American rodents called capybara, monkeys, and more from the deck as we passed.

At night, we'd tie up to the riverbank. Several evenings, we went out in the small boats after dark to explore, using a spotlight to find caimans on the banks, their eyes gleaming red in the light. Bats and owls flew overhead and dove close to snatch up insects drawn to the steering lights.

The best nighttime moment took place in a small, placid stream deep in the rainforest. Our guides switched off the spotlights and outboard motors of our boats so we could sit in silence and take in the night sounds of the Amazon in all their glory. The primeval thrill of hearing that wild cacophony of frogs, insects, and nocturnal birds on a moonless night in one of the most remote spots on Earth is difficult to adequately put into words. Today, years later, I shiver in delight as I write about the experience.

We enjoyed the small-boat voyage on the Amazon so much that we've since taken other small watercraft journeys in Alaska's Inside Passage and Glacier Bay and the waters of the Great Bear Rainforest of British Columbia. Small ships, with comparatively shallow drafts, can navigate narrow inlets and sail closer to shore than big cruise ships. In Glacier Bay, we got so close to the calving glaciers we could hear the crack when big chunks of ice broke off and tumbled into the water. We were never in danger but thrilled to watch the resulting waves rise and rush toward the boat. On our Great Bear Rainforest cruise, our restored tugboat eased so close to waterfalls we felt the spray on our faces.

The itineraries on small boat cruises are very loose, so if the crew sees a pod of whales or a grizzly on the beach, the ship's captain can pause and take advantage of the moment. On both trips, we zipped around in small Zodiacs, hiked on shore, and got up close and personal with whales, seals, bears, and other wildlife. Another rare treat was seeing pods of whales "bubble hunt" by circling their prey with a net of bubbles.

Mike and I have also taken two river cruises, one from Paris to Normandy, and one on the Danube through Hungary, Austria, Slovakia, and Germany. The biggest advantage of a river cruise is that we docked and explored a new place every day but only needed to unpack once. They also feed you lavishly and offer excursions to interesting places inland from the river. One of the most moving ceremonies I've ever witnessed took place during the Paris-to-Normandy cruise at the American Cemetery at Normandy. Those on hand to greet us emphasized that the people of Normandy still hold the American people in their hearts for our sacrifice on D-Day. A handful of our fellow passengers, World War II vets, were overcome with emotion at returning to the beaches where they fought and lost compatriots. My father and Mike's uncle both survived the Normandy invasion and the battles in France. His father fought in Belgium and elsewhere in Europe. Touring the beaches and seeing the lethal placement of the German gun batteries and difficult terrain put the Allied landing in sobering perspective. I have tears in my eyes again as I write about our visit.

On that river cruise, we also saw sights like Monet's home at Giverny with the iconic arched bridge featured in the famed Impressionist's paintings. Walking the streets of Paris and sitting in cafés on the Rive Gauche and elsewhere can never get old for me, so we made sure we had time for wandering the city. On the Danube cruise and its extension, I found the cities of Budapest and Prague everything and more than I expected from reading spy novels from such masters as John Le Carré, Robert Ludlum, and Daniel Silva. I could imagine a spy fleeing down the cities' timeworn streets or jumping a passing barge in their central rivers.

The only drawback to a river cruise is the number of passengers. The Viking Ships we traveled held roughly 150 passengers, several of whom we got to know at shared meals and during the excursions. But that number felt a bit too crowded for Mike and me, especially with the fleet of buses necessary to transport all the passengers on inland excursions.

So, with our frequent travel companions Steve and Betty Wing, we decided to downsize and try a barge cruise on France's Burgundy Canal. We had the *Magnolia* to ourselves, pampered by a five-person crew, including the chef. *C'etait magnifique!* The chef served us gourmet meals on board, including escargots and an elaborate *Boeuf Bourguignonne* that we helped him shop for in a village along the way. Dining on snails while drifting down a canal by barge must be the ultimate embrace of the slow food movement.

Two of the nights, we took our meals at restaurants near the canal. One evening, the captain's wife's parents hosted us in their home. Despite some language barriers, we managed to communicate quite well.

The beauty of a barge cruise is that the boat travels at such a leisurely pace it forces passengers to slow down and enjoy each moment. The Burgundy Canal, like most in Europe, has a series of locks that the boat must navigate. Clearing each lock takes about a half-hour while the captain waits for the water level in the lock to raise or lower the boat (depending upon direction traveled) so it can continue the journey. That meant we could ride the barge's bicycles on the path along the canal or into the small villages we passed for an hour or more and still beat the barge to the next lock. Or just laze on the deck with a book and another cool drink.

During the days, the captain's wife/activities director drove us to some of Burgundy's castles, vineyards, wineries, and villages. We even spent a morning walking through the woods watching a truffle-hunting dog nose out a basketful of the prized fungi. The truffle hunt was followed by a lunch heavy on truffle-laced dishes—even ice cream. No matter how expensive and sought-after truffles are as a flavoring in gourmet dishes, I can attest that ice cream and truffles were not meant for each other. But the other dishes were intriguing and tasty.

We've spent time on so many small boats I'm not sure I can remember them all. We've viewed birds and game, big and small, from boats on Uganda's Nile River, Botswana's Chobe and Linyanti Rivers, Zimbabwe's Zambezi River, and several places in Costa Rica. In Nepal, Vietnam, Laos, Myanmar, and Cambodia, we've taken boats to temples, floating villages and markets, and out-of-the-way caves. On Iceland's southeast coast, we rode a duck boat from land into the Jökulsárlón glacial lagoon to float among icebergs. Exhausted from several weeks on safari, Mike and I once spent an entire day just riding on boats through the canals of Amsterdam. We hopped off occasionally to take in a sight or have lunch, but most of our time was spent on the canals. We also enjoyed the canals of Venice. Our hotel sat on the Grand Canal, and we took several water taxis during our stay. And how could we spend time in Venice without the obligatory gondola ride? How lovely to wend through the smaller canals in the dark of night, listening to the whispers of this ancient, romantic city.

With our son, we kayaked the sea near Kaikoura on New Zealand's South Island. I found my only attempt at ocean kayaking a challenge with the waves, the currents, and the seals that kept trying to climb onto my kayak. Near the end of the trip, our guide tied my kayak to his and helped boost me back to shore. Still, it was an exhilarating experience—one I don't regret.

Mike and I also kayaked the icy waters of Alaska's Glacier Bay, surrounded by small icebergs that had calved from the active glaciers at the head of the bay. We paddled close—but not too close—to that glacier, riding the swells created as huge blocks of ice slipped into the water, each with a thunderous crack. Although the experience was fun, we had to be very cautious since a spill into the frigid water would have resulted in instant hypothermia. That afternoon's kayaking also brought us some unexpected amusement. At one point, we paddled by a huge cruise ship, and passengers lined up on deck to wave like we were part of the entertainment. We waved back, happy to become part of the passengers' Glacier Bay experience.

"Boats on Phewa Tal" by Sherry Knowlton. Pokhara, Nepal. 2011

In a warmer part of the world, Mike and I were the audience for a different kind of boat show. Our Bangkok hotel window framed a constant parade of ferries and water taxis, busy all day and night taking people from one side of the Chao Phraya River to the other. Later in our stay, we experienced the river-level view as we toured some of the sprawling city by canal boat. We passed giant monitor lizards basking on canal walls, tooled by houses that sat right on the water, and observed residents lounging on their porches and using the canals as their route to work. That water trip gave us a better perspective on the lives of many who call Thailand's sprawling capital city home.

From Krabi, on Thailand's southern beaches, Mike and I hired a longtail boat, a brightly decorated traditional boat with a hooked prow, to take us to several of the small islands in the Andaman Sea for the day. Some of the isles have beaches, but nearly all of them are dominated by lush hills that rise steeply out of the sea. At one island, our boatman took us through a narrow crevasse between two rugged limestone cliffs and into a "secret" lagoon hidden by the high peaks. The water inside was shallow and a great place to cool off with a swim. Touring the scattered islands allowed us to take in more of this beautiful area than the thin slice we'd admired from our beach chairs.

Sometimes the best way to travel from spot A to B is via ferry, which many regard less as an adventure and more as a mundane vehicle for commuting. To be fair, if a ferry is your floating version of a daily subway to work, the ride might lose its excitement. However, I almost always look forward to ferry rides. For me, they are something out of the ordinary, can provide a different perspective on travel, and—best of all—they get me out on the water. Our crossing from Vancouver to Victoria Island was smooth, with the occasional dolphin leaping beside the boat. The ferry to Ocracoke on the Outer Banks is always fun. When my college roommates and I meet in New York City, one of our favorite treats is riding the New York City ferry system. It's a relaxing way to get around the city, and the view of the city skyline from the Hudson River is outstanding.

A day wending our way slowly through the reed-fringed channels of Botswana's Okavango Delta by motorboat felt like paradise, especially while watching elephants, hippos, and leaping antelope-like red lechwe. Tearing across the choppy waters of Awaroa Bay on the way to our lodging in New Zealand's Abel Tasman National Park, I laughed out loud as the spray drenched us all. I felt the same exhilaration one night in the lagoon of Bora Bora, an island in French Polynesia. Our sailing captain picked us up in the boat's dinghy from a restaurant on a small atoll. As we sped out over the dark water, the skies opened, and it poured. We could do nothing except laugh and enjoy the rush as we motored through the stormy night back to our boat.

On the more serene side of boating, a mokoro ride must be the ultimate. Mike and I have often been passengers in these flat-bottomed, long canoes. All we had to do was sit back and watch birds, dragonflies, tiny frogs, and water lilies slide by at water level as our guide stood on the stern of the boat and poled us through the shallows of the Okavango Delta. Pure bliss. Another way to experience wildlife up close is a raft ride on the Snake River in the Tetons. We always select the early morning peaceful float—no rapids—and have seen moose, elk, beaver, eagles, and more as they come to the water to drink.

We got to experience serenity in a much larger package when Mike, Josh, and I spent a night on a small boat in Milford Sound. This fjord is one of the most gorgeous places on earth—a must-see for visitors to New Zealand's South Island. The sound can be packed with sightseers during the day. But at night, most visitors leave the area. Our twelve-passenger boat and one other anchored far apart in this huge expanse of silent water. Around us on three sides towered mountain slopes so steep we couldn't see the peaks from water level. In the morning, the chattering of small Fiordland crested penguins and puffins broke the morning calm. After breakfast, we reluctantly returned to the real world following our night of natural peace.

Entranced by travel magazine photos, I'd looked forward for years to our overnight boat trip on Ha Long Bay off the coast of northern Vietnam. To get there, we drove for several hours through depressing industrial cities and small towns, many of them black with grime from the tall smokestacks we passed. The area reminded me of the United States in the days before we instituted pollution control and other environmental regulations. But, when we arrived at Ha Long Bay, all that ugliness disappeared. We spent a day and night on a traditional-style junk that slept fewer than twenty. The bay itself has been featured on many magazines and postcards, its calm waters punctuated by limestone karsts that rise forty feet into the air. To call the bay picturesque is a total understatement. It's breathtakingly beautiful.

I rose early to join a Tai Chi class on deck. What a serene way to greet the morning—Tai Chi exercises that began in a mist-shrouded bay and proceeded until the vapor gave way to the rosy glow of breaking dawn. We took small rowboats from the junk to visit a floating village, a pearl farm, and the huge Hang Sửng Sốt ("Surprise Caves") on one of the bay's larger islands.

Not every boating experience has been perfect. As foolish new parents, Mike and I took our son camping in Maine shortly after his first birthday. We slept in the small tent we'd used for backpacking. One morning, we decided to take a day sail on a schooner from Bar Harbor. The weather turned bad at sea, and Mike spent most of the trip below deck with a wailing baby. The camping experiment didn't turn out much better. After a few difficult days, we packed up the tent and finished out the week in a small cabin with beds and a kitchen. It was years before we tried camping or boating with Josh again.

Another boat trip gone wrong took place in Uganda's Queen Elizabeth National Park, where we spent hours waiting for a ferry to be fixed so we could return to camp. The ferry, the only way across the river, consisted of a few boards wide enough for four vehicles slapped onto a pontoon undercarriage and propelled by an ancient diesel engine. The diesel went kaput, and the ferry operator had to call civilization for a part to repair it. We whiled away the time by watching a family of baboons try to steal food from the steadily mounting group of waiting passengers and listening to a local drum band play to the largest audience they'd probably had in years.

That Ugandan ferry wasn't the only one we had trouble with. We once took the commercial ferry from St. Vincent to Bequia on high seas. After an hour of bouncing, my stomach was desperate to get off that boat. That brush with seasickness stayed with me for years, so memorable that when we returned to Bequia almost two decades later, I breathed a sigh of relief to find that we could arrive by small plane instead of the ferry.

Back to the not-quite-what-you-expected category of boat rides: In a small group tour of Costa Rica, we chose optional activities one afternoon. Mike went zip-lining through the rainforest canopy. Our friend Steve and I were looking for something less adventurous, so we decided upon a float trip. Assured that this was the gentle version of the available raft trips, some of which involved whitewater, we took our cameras to photograph the scenery and wildlife. Our first clue should have been that moment when the river guide took our cameras and packed them into a dry bag. He said he'd pass them to us at any point we wanted to take a photo. Then he assisted us in donning heavy-duty life vests and helmets. Helmets?

The trip in the rubber raft started out peacefully enough, although the current was swift. Only a few minutes later, we hit our first rapids. Granted, they weren't Class IV or Class V. Our guide did all the paddling, but still, I had to hold on to avoid falling out of the raft as we picked up speed and bounced over rocks. I could have left my camera behind since I needed both hands just to stay in the boat. Thank heavens for the dry bags, as the bottom of the raft was soon filled with water.

On the third set of rapids, the boat lurched against a submerged boulder and Steve, who was sitting next to me near the prow, toppled off his seat on the side of the raft and backward into the water. He managed to hold on with both hands to the rope that circled the boat. But his head dipped underwater as the boat accelerated down the river. Gravity and the erratic motion of the boat over rapids made it impossible for him to scramble back into the raft. I grabbed his life vest and helped keep his face above water until the guide was able to steer us to the shallows, jump out, and help my friend back into the boat. Steve was fine. But both of us felt the aftereffects of straining unused muscles the next day. By the time we left Costa Rica, we could laugh about the frightening experience, a reminder that danger can come from nowhere in a split second.

Our son has taken several trips down the Cheat and the New Rivers in West Virginia when the rapids were running at Class IV. He loved the rush. But my Costa Rica experience, tame in comparison, was more than enough for me to check off "running rapids" on my lifetime to-do list. I have no desire to go above the Costa Rican version of Class I again.

Despite a handful of bad experiences, I rarely miss a chance to step onto a boat. This chapter and the next just skim the surface of my time spent on creeks, ponds, rivers, lakes, and oceans. Like Norman Maclean writes in *A River Runs Through It and Other Stories*, I, too, am "haunted by waters."[3]

---

3 Norman Maclean, *A River Runs Through It and Other Stories* (Chicago: University of Chicago Press, 1976), 161.

6

Sailing

I CAN'T REMEMBER a time I didn't long to sail, but I'd passed well into adulthood before I got the chance to try. Why sailing? Because I love being on the water. Because there's something both serene and adventurous about a boat under sail. Perhaps I succumbed to the subliminal message from that Tennyson quote on my bedroom bulletin board: "For my purpose holds to sail beyond the sunset, and the baths of all the western stars, until I die." But I've often wondered if finding that quote as a preteen inspired my interest in sailing, or did an early attraction to sailing make that quote catch my eye?

Before I ever stepped onto the deck of a sailboat, I devoured books like *Mutiny on the Bounty* and *Kon-tiki*. One of my favorite series as a young adult was John D. MacDonald's Travis McGee books. Granted, McGee lived on a houseboat, not a sailboat, but the books were imbued with a tropical vibe. Later I was captivated by Stuart Woods's early novel, *Run Before the Wind*, where his protagonist, Will Lee, does some serious trans-Atlantic sailing. And, after we started to sail ourselves, I became hooked on a limited series of suspenseful adventures by Paul Garrison that involve daring escapes by sailboat. From the profusion of books about life under sail, it's obvious many authors share my fascination with the sea. I love the interactive relationship between a good book on a subject of interest like sailing and people who love the pastime. Books inspire sailors. Sailors write books, and those inspire more sailors. Delightful.

Growing up in landlocked Southcentral Pennsylvania, I had no opportunities for sailing during my childhood. The closest I ever got to

"Old Sailor" by Mike Knowlton. Bequia, St. Vincent and the Grenadines. 2018

a sailboat was seeing a few in the distance at the Jersey Shore or in the harbor at Connecticut's Mystic Seaport on a trip with Grandma Anne. When Mike and I took our journey across America, we saw many sailboats on Cape Cod, Maine, and the Pacific Coast. But we had no spare cash for sailing trips. And for the next few years, mountain trails still held us firmly in their grip.

Our first trip to the Caribbean, camping in the national park on the US Virgin Island of St. John and a few days in Puerto Rico, loosened the mountains' hold. The seductive lure of white sand beaches and turquoise waves reeled us in. We enjoyed the swimming and snorkeling, the balmy air and little beach bars. Soon after, we returned to the Virgin Islands with a stay on St. Thomas. Then the birth of our son and that disastrous first-birthday vacation with him in Maine shifted us into a more sedate approach to travel for the time being. With toddler Josh, we began to vacation in the Outer Banks, a place we've returned to regularly over the past four decades for its beauty and accessible, family-friendly beaches.

During Josh's early years, Mike and I once left him at home in the care of Aunt Linda while we returned to St. Thomas for a lovely beach getaway. There we ventured out in a small sailboat for the very first time. To an outside observer, that day sail would not have been remarkable. All around the Caribbean, tourists take day sails and sunset cruises three hundred sixty-five days of the year. We sailed. The captain anchored so we could snorkel and swim. We sampled tropical drinks. But for us, that excursion opened the door to a whole new world. With that ordinary little day sail, Mike and I crossed a threshold. Despite my frequent prodding, he'd been reluctant to try sailing because, as a child, he'd been prone to motion sickness. Mike expected a queasy stomach on an ocean sail. Turns out, he was just fine on the ocean. No stomach problems at all. And we both loved the sailing experience.

From that time on, we started to explore other Caribbean Islands. Once or twice on our own, then with school-age Josh in tow, we spent our vacation time on St. Martin, St. Thomas, St. Lucia, and Tortola in the British Virgin Islands. Each time, we'd make sure we had one day-sail in our itinerary. Finally, when Josh was eight, we stayed at our favorite hotel on Tortola, the Sugar Mill, but spent the final five days of our trip on a chartered sailboat cruise around the British Virgin Islands (BVIs). Richard and Vanessa, a young British couple with a small child, were our captain and crew on *Dream On*. We visited the famous Foxy's beach bar on Jost Van Dyke and added our dollar bill to the wall. We anchored within hailing distance of Sir Richard Branson's private Necker Island and discovered the Baths on Virgin Gorda. The Baths, a rock formation that visitors can climb and swim through, look as if a careless giant stopped at the edge of the pristine beach and emptied his pockets of huge boulders. My best memory of that trip is sitting on deck one night while at anchor in a small cove, no other boats around, just listening to the quiet.

On our next sailing adventure, we again chartered. This time we chose a cruise through the southern Caribbean with Russell and Evelyn, a South African couple. Mike, Josh, and I boarded the *Anne Marie II*, a 47-foot Hinckley, in Bequia and sailed south through the Grenadines, disembarking two weeks later in Canouan.

Several of the islands in this part of the Windward chain are absolute gems. Tiny Mayreau featured a rustic beachfront hotel and a single road we followed over the mountain to the small village on the far side. In the morning, we awoke to the sounds of a braying donkey racing up and down the hill near our anchorage. We stopped for lunch at the private island enclave of Petit St. Vincent, which caters to vacationers seeking seclusion. Guests run a flag up a pole at their cottage to indicate they're ready to have staff service their room. We even spent a few hours one afternoon sunning and swimming on an uninhabited speck of perfect white sand graced by a single palm—our own private island.

The crowning jewel of the Grenadines, the archipelago known as the Tobago Cays, was fringed by pristine beds of coral. With little yacht traffic, only a handful of other boats passed by in the distance while we stopped to snorkel. The deserted anchorage felt like a perfect slice of paradise. The main sign that other humans had visited were conch shells piled in tiny pyramids on the surrounding islets.

Our captain, Russell, welcomed our interest in helping with the boat, so he taught the Knowlton family how to raise and lower the sails, catch the wind, anchor, and many other intricacies of sailing. We returned home as a family anxious to learn to sail on our own. Thus, we embarked on a multi-year series of learn-to-sail courses at the Annapolis Sailing School on the Chesapeake, a few hours from our home. Mike, Josh, and I together progressed from elementary classes to advanced certification. All were done on the Chesapeake, some involving days and nights on the water with our instructors. We learned how to trim (adjust) a sail for the wind, anchor and dock, steer with both a tiller and wheel, navigate and read charts, tie nautical knots, and much more.

With sufficient expertise to sail independently, we chartered boats from an Annapolis company for long weekends on the Chesapeake and explored the charming small towns of Maryland's Eastern Shore like St. Michaels. Our trips ashore included dinners at local crab houses, where the staff would deliver buckets of hard-shells along with a mallet so patrons could crack them open on newspaper-covered picnic tables. Dotted with squat octagonal lighthouses unique to the area, the Chesapeake's short reaches, quiet inlets, and sheltered coves provide an ideal training area for beginning sailors.

One of my best memories of any trip we've ever taken comes from an early fall morning on a deserted inlet on the Wye River, where we'd anchored for the night. When I opened the boat's hatch and climbed out onto the deck, a thick mist shrouded the entire area. The air reverberated with a muffled chorus of waterfowl sounds. Huge flocks of migrating ducks and geese that had touched down during the night were quacking and honking to greet the dawn. Floating amid all those waterfowl felt both surreal and serene. I couldn't see them through the hovering mist, but I could tell that hundreds, maybe thousands, of birds surrounded the boat. By the time we raised anchor, the rising sun had burned off the mist, and most of the birds had taken wing, headed south for the winter.

Our final Annapolis Sailing School course took us back to the Virgin Islands. The three of us had an instructor/captain for the weeklong course, a genial and knowledgeable guy named Roger. We boarded our fifty-foot sailboat in St. Croix in the US Virgins and sailed to St. John and through much of the BVIs. With good weather and calm seas, we enjoyed the sailing and learned a lot. Despite the heavy emphasis on the engine maintenance that's critical to keeping instruments running and motoring when conditions aren't suitable for sail, we all managed to earn our cruising certification.

By now, twelve-year-old Josh had become an avid and skilled sailor, but Mom hadn't anticipated some of the other learning experiences he encountered on that trip. One evening, we anchored by a floating restaurant near the bight off Norman Island in the BVIs. The old ship, the *William Thornton*, taken out of mothballs and repurposed into a restaurant, was fondly known by the yachting crowd as the *Willy T*. The food was fair to middling, but Josh was more interested in the action at the bar. A series of young women took turns lying on the bar for their boyfriends to drink belly shots off their bare, whipped-creamed midriffs. A cosmopolitan experience for a preteen from a tiny rural town, even for the nineties.

I'll note that the hurricanes of 2017 destroyed the *Willy T* we'd visited on those early sails. That ship now sits on the BVI seabed, sunk by the government to create an artificial reef. But the owners found and repurposed a new boat, christened it the *William Thornton*, and put it in operation as a restaurant at Norman Island. Mike and I saw the new *Willy T* in 2020 on a day cruise around the BVIs, but we didn't stop. The place was still hopping, and I understand that belly shots are still a popular visitor pastime.

One of the highlights of our sailing years was a charter through the Greek Islands. I had been fascinated by Greece ever since those high school days when I'd read *The Moonspinners*. Then my college English classes included the classic Greek tragedies and comedies and novels like *Zorba the Greek* and John Fowler's *The Magus*. The country and its islands had always been at the top of my places-to-visit list. Knowing about my longing for a trip to Greece, Mike gave me the most romantic anniversary gift ever for our twenty-fifth wedding anniversary. Unbeknownst to me, he'd been saving money for a trip to Greece, including a sail through the Cyclades Islands.

Josh, then fourteen, came with us. After spending several days touring the Parthenon, the Plaka, and the other sights of Athens, we made our way to the coast and our yacht. Our captain, a Brit named Billy, was the only shadow on the trip. The guy was a jerk who relished his authority a bit more than any other charter yacht captain we'd met. But he did take us on a glorious cruise, starting with three of the Saronic Islands just below the tip of Greece's mainland: Poros, Hydra, and Spetses. Then we sailed and sometimes motored east to the Cyclades, the islands usually featured in photos of Greece. Whitewashed houses with cobalt and turquoise shutters clinging to steep hills. Gorgeous flowers climbing every wall. Azure skies so blue they take one's breath away. Yes, those islands.

We visited Mykonos, island of windmills and decadent all-night parties, the antiquity-filled Delos, and a series of smaller, lesser-known islands like Kea, Syros, and Serifos. Along the way, we trudged up or caught taxis to each island's mountaintop village, called the *hora*. We sat on pebbly beaches and swam in the buoyant, high salt-content water. We wandered through narrow streets and ate fresh seafood in quayside tavernas. On one island, we watched villagers leap over a burning fire to celebrate St. John's Eve as part of an annual ritual to cleanse themselves of evil. Josh furthered his worldly education with an introduction to a common practice of European women: topless sunbathing.

In the Caribbean and many other areas of the world, sailboats anchor or tie up at buoys offshore, and passengers take a dinghy to the dock. Many places also have marinas where sailors pay for a slip to dock their boats. In Greece, however, European docking is the norm: sailboats lash to each other with just a row of rubber fenders to keep the hulls apart. In several of the ports we visited, boats nestled against each other, three or four deep. Latecomers just tied up to the nearest boat's stern and walked across neighboring boats' decks until they reached land.

This practice allows everyone to dock in a popular harbor, but crowding expensive yachts together can also lead to some conflict. On the quiet little island of Kea, we docked at a great spot on the quay, just steps from a lovely taverna. However, next door was a boatload of Germans who hadn't deployed their fenders correctly. When the waves kept slamming their boat against ours, Captain Billy tore into a multi-lingual shouting match with the drunken young men. It didn't quite come to blows but could have. Later, we sat near each other in the restaurant at dinner, and, perhaps a bit more sober, the Germans apologized.

On the island of Serifos, our fifty-foot yacht was one of the smaller boats at the long double row of docks. But our berth gave us a front-row seat to the collision between two giant luxury motor yachts when an incoming vessel cut too close while turning into its slip. Everyone from the docked yacht and the incoming yacht, both crewed, multi-level, and well over a hundred feet long, poured out on deck and started screaming at each other. The damage likely wouldn't prevent either watercraft from sailing, but when a boat costs millions of dollars, even crumpled trim on the stern is no small thing. We later learned that the offending yacht carried some Hollywood types. In a local taverna that evening, we encountered one of the passengers, Dennis Franz of *Hill Street Blues* fame.

Although we sailed many more times in the Caribbean and the Chesapeake, our last distant sailing adventure was a romantic getaway for Mike and me in French Polynesia. We stayed on the island of Moorea for a few days in an overwater bungalow and ended our trip in another overwater bungalow on Tahiti. In between, we spent ten days sailing through the islands of Bora Bora, Huahine, Raiatea, and Taha'a. We needed a captain who knew the local waters for this trip, which involved both long-distance sailing between islands and entering the dangerous rings of coral and atoll chains that circle each of the main islands. Our captain, Pierre, a Frenchman, had sailed the islands for years and knew the best spots to snorkel and explore as well as all the great restaurants.

The Society Islands are truly magnificent. It's easy to understand why the *Bounty*'s mutineers became entranced with the South Pacific. (If it's been a while since you've read the book or seen the movie, the crew and second-in-command of the Royal Navy ship *Bounty* mutinied against their commander, Captain Bligh, partly because of his harsh discipline but also because they'd succumbed to the siren call of the women and easy living of Polynesia.)

We spent several days on secluded and empty beaches fringed with palms, where our captain (an amiable guy with none of the characteristics of Captain Bligh) would drop us off with a picnic lunch. We snorkeled the coral reefs to view bright tropical fish and yellow-tipped reef sharks (allegedly harmless but a little scary all the same). We sampled rustic beach restaurants and fancy resort hotel dining. Our best meal was on a tiny atoll on the edge of one of the lagoons. The islander and his wife, who lived alone on the islet, prepared a fresh fish dinner over an open fire, which we ate in a tiny thatched pavilion at sunset.

At the peak of our sailing days, Mike and I made plans to buy our own sailboat and spend months exploring the Caribbean when we retired. I poured over sailing magazines, comparing models of boats to determine which were best suited to long-term living. But there were other sights in the world we wanted to see. And, when Josh went off to college, we decided it was time to visit some of those places instead of spending every vacation sailing. As we sampled other parts of the world, our sailing dreams faded.

I don't regret the change in course. In our travels, we've still found new ways to experience time on the water. And we've discovered satisfying adventures on land, ones we might have missed if we'd tethered ourselves long-term to a sailing yacht.

Learning to sail as a family was an excellent way to spend time with our growing son. Between the time on the road for his travel hockey and the spring/summer sailing trips, we spent much more time with him than many parents do with kids of that age. Recently, Josh, his wife, Laura, and our granddaughter, joined us for an island vacation on St. John. Mike and I couldn't have been happier when Josh and Laura told us they planned to round up some friends for a sailing trip soon—carrying on the Knowlton tradition.

I suspect my days on small sailboats are all in the past. I'm no longer nimble enough to scamper to the prow to drop anchor quickly or strong enough to raise and cleat a sail in high winds. Even with the new automated winches and other equipment that make sailing much less labor-intensive, I don't believe I'm physically up to the challenge. But I loved every minute of our sailing days, even the times we beat through gusty winds and pouring rain. Even the times we anchored in a bay with a running swell that rocked the boat so hard the rigging rattled all night long. Even the times I searched the horizon desperately for a glimpse of land to stave off the seasickness I could feel building during a rough passage.

We chartered our last yacht more than a decade ago for another sail through the BVIs. Yet, all these years later, when I need a moment of calm or a focus for mediation, I imagine myself in a sailboat at the instant when the motor shuts down and the peace begins: That hushed symphony of wind and water that is the world under sail.

"Maraya, the Blackback Gorilla" by Mike Knowlton. Bwindi Impenetrable Forest, Uganda. 2013

Amazing Wildlife Experiences

I N MANY ways, each day in a new country, a new place, a new situation is an amazing experience. One of the reasons I so love to travel is the thrill of anticipation and the surprise of the unfamiliar. To be completely honest, not all that travel brings is terrific. Trips can be tiring. Plans can go awry. People, whether fellow travelers or those you meet along the way, can be a pain. But for me, all those irritations vanish when I experience something unique that I could only have encountered through travel. Many of my most memorable experiences have been with wildlife. Not surprising, since I've always liked nature, spending time outdoors, and seeing wild animals in their environments.

On our sail through the Society Islands of French Polynesia, Mike and I anchored one night on the far side of Bora Bora at a spot in the lagoon known for manta ray activity. The gentler cousins to stingrays, mantas have no barbs with which to sting humans or other creatures. Early the next morning, we snorkeled from the sailboat, slipping into the warm water from the stern. A soft rain fell over the lagoon, blurring the line between gray water and gray sky. When we first entered the lagoon, we simply enjoyed the spectacular array of bright tropical fish surrounding us. Next, we spent several minutes evading a barracuda that had developed a strong interest in Mike.

No sooner had we ditched the barracuda when, out of the depths of the lagoon, a giant shadow came sweeping toward us, its huge wings gracefully undulating. We dove beneath the water to meet this beautiful creature head-on. The graceful manta ray drew steadily nearer until only a few feet separated us. Its wingspan, twelve feet or more, framed a tiny squarish head. Below the lagoon's surface in the manta's world, the three of us came face-to-face—probably just for a few seconds, but it seemed a moment frozen in time. Pure magic. The hush of the briny water. The light filtering from above. Most riveting, the imperturbable gaze of this gentle ocean mammoth.

Another manta emerged from the deep, and our companion glided away. We headed to the surface for air. The spell had broken, but the memory of that mystical moment in the waters of Bora Bora will be with me as long as I live.

I'll admit it. I get a kick out of swimming with gentle aquatic creatures. In Tulum, Mexico, we went to a water park, a much more low-key version of the thrill-a-minute, giant sliding board places we think of as water parks in the States. Instead, Xel Ha's design echoed the natural feeling of the *cenotes*, the many sinkholes that dot the limestone bedrock of the Yucatán Peninsula. The highlight of our time there was a swim with dolphins in a lake-sized saltwater pool.

In recent years, animal rights groups have raised ethical questions about keeping dolphins and whales in captivity and exploiting them for tourism. Our swim with these captive dolphins was well before that point of view became more prevalent, but I must admit that the dolphin interaction was an exhilarating experience.

We petted the dolphins and played with them for most of the hour. I was surprised at the leathery texture of their skins. Perhaps the slickness of water on their backs when they leap out of the sea creates an illusion, but I had expected them to have soft exteriors. Near the end of the session, Mike, Josh, and I each paired with a dolphin that put its nose on the soles of our feet and propelled us at a dizzying speed across the water. I can still remember the hard curve of the mammal's snout against my instep as we flew over the water's surface. It was great fun. If you feel the need for speed, dolphin propulsion is a great way to go.

We had a very different type of interaction with wild dolphins in the Amazon River basin. When we cruised the Peruvian Amazon on a small ship, the guides told us time and again that the waters of the Amazon were as dangerous as they were murky. The waters were not suitable for swimming unless, like the Ribereño families who lived on the river, one had developed resistance to the river's bacteria and knew how to avoid some of the creatures that lurk beneath the surface.

However, as we moved farther upstream into the Pacaya Samiria Reserve, we traveled on smaller and smaller tributaries that fed the larger Amazon. Some of these rivers were blackwater rivers, which ran dark but clear and bacteria-free due to tannins from decayed vegetation. On one of those blackwater rivers, we jumped into the water to swim with the pink dolphins that had been following the boat. Yes, pink dolphins.

These freshwater dolphins, which live in South American rivers, have skin the same shade of blush pink found inside many seashells. They look like rosy wraiths as they slip through the water, leaping above the surface from time to time. These wild creatures were warier of Mike, me, and our fellow boaters than the habituated dolphins of Xel Ha. Nonetheless, they circled our group and swam among us, their bulbous heads and long beaks making them appear as if they were smiling all the while.

On two of our cruises, one to Alaska's Glacier Bay and Inside Passage, and one to the waters of British Columbia's Great Bear Rainforest, we saw whales. As our small ships motored through the mostly calm waters, we encountered pod after pod of humpbacks and orcas. Several times we got very close to the giant humpbacks at water-level, so close we could smell from our Zodiacs the fishy odor as the graceful mammals spouted through their blowholes then dove below the surface. One of the most startling whale encounters came on the deck of our ship in Glacier Bay. The captain had spotted a pod of humpbacks from the upper cockpit, and we were on deck, all eyes looking to port for the whales to surface again. Just then, we heard a splash behind us and turned to see a colossal humpback breaching less than twenty feet from the ship. The mammal leaped into the air, tail dancing on the surface, before its entire length crashed back into the water, creating a splash so humongous it rocked the whole boat.

Another awe-inspiring water encounter, this one involving land animals, took place in Zimbabwe. At Little Makalolo in Hwange National Park, the camp has constructed an observation blind next to a shallow pond. We spent several hours late one afternoon sitting in this animal viewing area, watching herds of elephants drink from the pool. The blind, constructed of downed trees with a space in the middle to sit, provided openings wide enough to watch the animals and take photos. Screened by the logs, we stayed quiet as we observed the herd. The massive beasts, which came within a few feet of the structure, paid us no heed and went about their activities without fear. We shot some spectacular pictures of several elephant families in the water.

In another incredible wildlife experience, this one on dry ground, we had a fascinating encounter with a wild Bengal tiger. Arrowhead, as she was dubbed by the guides of India's Ranthambhore National Park, was not our first tiger sighting. We'd been to India before and saw several tigers, mainly at a distance in Bandhavgarh and Kanha parks. Others we saw from elephant-back were closer but snoozing in the underbrush.

So, on our second trip to India, this time with friends Betty and Steve, we worked with a private guide, Narendra Sharma, to design a tiger safari. We visited the Taj Mahal and other cultural sites, but we focused on tigers in the wild. On our first stop, Ranthambhore, we saw several tigers, including Arrowhead herself, in the early days of our stay. Thrilling, to be sure. But often, those tigers were distant or surrounded by several other vehicles.

We spent all our safari time in the national parks riding in the Indian equivalent of topless jeeps. I don't remember the brand name, but they were smaller than the old US Army-type jeep, with seats for the driver and another passenger in the front and four to five people crammed onto two bench seats in the back. Due to the danger from the tiger population, we were only allowed to step out of the vehicles at designated rest stations along the way. We had a flat tire at one park, and the guides had to change it with four of us sitting in the vehicle. If they'd let us hop out to lessen the weight—and were caught by a ranger—they could have lost their guide licenses. The great advantage of these small, open vehicles is that we had a 360-degree view of the jungle and other terrain. The downside is that the roads were so dusty that, in some places, we wore bandannas over our mouths and hats or scarves over our heads. A Lawrence of Arabia look minus the camel.

Lucky for us, we were able to enjoy much of our third day in Ranthambhore without worrying about the dust clouds thrown by other vehicles. Our guide, Narendra, had secured a special pass for our group of four that allowed us to stay in the park for the entire day. Most visitors were required to leave the park at ten in the morning and could only return at two in the afternoon. Park management strove to lessen the disruption to the animals in the midday heat, so only a few vehicles could obtain the full-access pass on any given day. We had the entire park almost to ourselves for those four late morning and early afternoon hours.

During that time, we discovered Arrowhead swimming across a wide lake. We followed her at a distance by jeep as she emerged from the water, shook like an immense dog, and made her way up a hill into the crumbling, overgrown ruins of an ancient building. We waited patiently for her to surface again. One of the constants of a tiger safari is waiting. In some parks, the jungle can be so thick that a tiger could be lying in the underbrush five feet away, yet it can't be seen from the road. So, often, we had to wait a long time for a tiger to emerge into the open. This day, we were lucky. Arrowhead soon left the ruins and continued her stroll. Narendra and the driver circled on the dusty, narrow track to a spot where they thought she'd emerge from the jungle. And she did. She slipped through the curtain of dense vegetation, strode to the side of the road no more than ten feet away, and sat down to groom.

There we were, alone in the jungle with a magnificent Bengal tiger. She seemed unbothered by the clicking of cameras as we all tried to capture the perfect photo. But the wildest part came about ten minutes later when the tiger rose and walked down the road, directly toward our vehicle. Our driver backed up a few feet at a time as she came nearer and nearer. Then he stopped as she strolled by, paying us little heed. She brushed by my side of the vehicle, passing so close I could have stroked her blazing fur with my palm.

What a magnificent animal. Her golden-orange coat glowed like fire in the midday sun. Most impressive—and more than a little frightening—was this lethal cat's size and power. Her back rose above the metal sides of the vehicle. She was roughly eight feet long from head to tail. Her paws as big as dinner plates. Called pug marks, the tracks she left behind in the dust brought home the beast's deadly capabilities. My heart shot to my throat as she padded by us, but to see a wild tiger that close ranks high in my list of thrilling experiences. We saw more tigers, even cubs, in Ranthambhore and the other parks we visited (twenty-two sightings in all) along with leopards, sun bears and sloth bears, peacocks, spotted deer, and the giant buffalo-type beasts called gaur. But that afternoon encounter with Arrowhead stands out.

The animal experience that most warms my heart took place in the Bwindi Impenetrable Forest. The safari in Uganda was unique from many of our other safaris, with less tourist infrastructure than other destinations we'd visited. Many of the camps could be called more spartan than rustic. We drove long distances on rough roads among several national parks, where animal populations had just begun to turn the corner after years of conflict, neglect, and poaching under dictator Idi Amin.

However, we saw beautiful Murchison Falls, completely open and barrier-free in the wilderness. (Imagine standing on the precipice of a 141-foot waterfall in the United States without guardrails, signs, or a park ranger!) We took boat trips to view water animals and birds, including the prehistoric-looking shoebill stork on the banks of the Nile. We trekked into the forest at Kibale to see a colony of chimpanzees living in their nests high among the treetops. And we stayed at a beautiful lodge perched on a narrow ridge in the Rwenzori Mountains, also known as the Mountains of the Moon. Emphasizing the property's colonial past, the approach to the luxury lodge wound through acres of tea plantations filled with workers harvesting the tender leaves.

But seeing mountain gorillas was our ultimate goal in Uganda. And so, our small group came to Bwindi, not far from the Uganda/Democratic Republic of the Congo border and one of the few places in the world to view mountain gorillas in the wild. Access to the gorillas is highly controlled to protect the endangered animals. Although there has been some slight growth in numbers over recent years, few more than one thousand remain on Earth. To see them, one must make a reservation and obtain a pricey permit months in advance. Trekkers gather at the park each morning to receive assignments, based on physical ability, for which of several habituated gorilla families they are permitted to seek out that day.

What a dream. To view gorillas in their natural habitat. However, our group had but a single day carved out in our itinerary to make the trek. When we arrived at Bwindi, we checked into our camp and went to bed early. We were scheduled to rise before dawn and drive to the trekkers' gathering point. But in the middle of the night, I became violently ill. I'll spare you the messy details, but I spent most of the night in the bathroom, coming to the devastating realization that there was no way I could hike to see gorillas. I was feeling so terrible that I could barely make it back to bed.

Mike dressed in the dark pre-dawn hours, hoping he would see a family of gorillas on the day's hike but worried about whether he should leave me while I was ill. I encouraged him to go—no reason for both of us to miss the gorillas.

He did see the elusive beasts. Because Mike was in great physical shape, he was assigned to a group of trekkers that spent seven hours hiking up, then back down, a steep, jungle-covered mountain in the sticky heat. A guide led the group and hacked through the vegetation with a machete. Another guide carried a gun to protect against wild elephants. And local porters helped each trekker by carrying their backpacks and boosting them up the incline in sections where the slope approached vertical. All the group's effort paid off when they located their family of gorillas, the Habinyanja group.

Mike was at the front of the group when the male silverback rushed through the underbrush and charged, stopping short just a few feet away. Before encountering the family, the guide had instructed Mike and the others to keep their eyes downcast to avoid challenging or upsetting a confrontational gorilla. After establishing that he was the main primate in this corner of the jungle, the big silverback turned his back on Mike and returned to his family.

For a strictly regulated hour, Mike's group sat and observed the gorilla family from a short distance. Bwindi's human visitors are not permitted to approach or interact with the gorillas to prevent the endangered animals from contracting human diseases. Of course, like the silverback that charged, the gorillas sometimes choose to interact with humans. Then, trekkers are instructed to just go with the flow. The gorilla family of nineteen that Mike visited included the big male, a younger blackback male, several females, and seven youngsters from baby to teenage. Several of the younger gorillas approached the group of humans, but none of them touched Mike or his companions.

Meanwhile, I still lay in bed, too sick at this point to even bemoan the fact that I'd come thousands of miles to see gorillas and missed my only chance. One of the room stewards at our camp took care of me, bringing me tea and broth that I failed to keep down and then trying to keep me hydrated with rehydration salts dissolved in water. But I got steadily worse. By early afternoon, I realized I was seriously ill and began wondering if there was any place nearby for a helicopter to land and airlift me back to a hospital in Entebbe.

When Mike arrived back at camp, still high on the bliss of the gorilla encounter, he learned that my intestinal issues had not improved. At that point, he, the camp management, and our expedition guide decided I needed medical treatment. Lucky for me, Bwindi has a community hospital. Originally founded by two Americans to care for the Batwa forest pygmies displaced when the Ugandan government designated the Bwindi Impenetrable Forest as a national park, the modest hospital is funded largely by international donors.

A doctor examined me in a small room, its windows open to the air, in a one-story wing of the hospital. After a blood test, he diagnosed me with septicemia, a dangerous blood infection (more widely known as sepsis). It's unclear how I got the infection. The doctor suggested that I could have ingested bacteria or absorbed it through a cut, even though I had followed all the strict rules of travel in exotic countries. But in the bush, eating picnic lunches prepared by local staff, touching contaminated surfaces, getting nicks and scrapes along the way, it's hard to stay completely safe.

The very competent young doctor gave me intravenous antibiotics and a saline drip for rehydration. Several hours later, he sent me back to camp with a box of antibiotic tablets, almost the last of the hospital's precious supply. When we paid the $35 that my life-saving treatment cost, the hospital gave me my medical record for the visit, written by hand in an old-school notebook, the kind that I wrote essays on in college. With the antibiotics, I could continue the safari.

The following day, our group checked out and walked to our two vehicles at the camp entrance. I was still feeling miserable but light years better than twenty-four hours earlier. Better enough to now be devasted by the fact that I'd come to Bwindi and hadn't seen a gorilla. Like Mike, all our safari group had seen gorillas the previous day, although most observed a smaller, more easily accessible family.

Just then, our guide, Edward, who had been cleaning the window of the lead vehicle, rushed back to me. "Come," he said. "But quietly." He motioned everyone else except for Mike to stay back and ushered me to a space in front of the cars. There, a family of gorillas emerged from the underbrush into a clearing, no more than twenty feet away. A silverback, a mama with a tiny baby clinging to her back, and five more gorillas of varying sizes. The silverback paused for a long moment to study us, then led the family up the hill into the forest.

Perhaps I can blame my weakened physical state, but I cried at the sight of the gorillas. Several of our fellow travelers, who'd crept close enough to witness the sighting, shed tears as well, overcome with joy for me. I didn't get to see these rare and endangered animals for a full hour, but at least I got a five-minute glimpse of mountain gorillas in their natural habitat—a safari miracle.

I learned later that Edward had broken the rules for me. Technically, tourists are not supposed to stop, view, or engage with the gorillas unless on a permitted trek. But he and the rest of my safari companions were thrilled that I had a chance to see these endangered animals I'd come so far to view. With the doctor's prescribed antibiotics, I recovered over the next several days as we finished the safari in Uganda. Then Mike and I flew south for another two weeks' safari in Botswana. When we arrived home, the Bwindi Community Hospital received another check from grateful international donors.

"Reticulated Giraffes" by Mike Knowlton. Samburu National Park, Kenya. 2007

8

Africa in My Blood

A N OLD saying popular in movies and often heard on our trips to Africa is that the continent gets "in your blood." And, no, I'm not talking about the septicemia, which quite literally did get in my blood in Uganda. I'm referring to something much less tangible. A feeling. A longing. From the moment of our first safari to Tanzania, a love of the entire experience—being in the bush, seeing so many fascinating animals, ripping around in SUVs and small boats, and just breathing the dust—captivated me.

In some ways, I believe I loved the African wild before I ever stepped foot on the continent. In his nonfiction memoir *Green Hills of Africa*, Ernest Hemingway, one of my favorite authors, wrote about lying awake at night in Africa, homesick and pining for the continent even before he'd left to return home. Reading this and the short Hemingway story, *The Snows of Kilimanjaro*, made me long to see Mt. Kilimanjaro and other parts of the continent. Other books by Robert Ruark, Wilbur Smith, Alan Patton, Alexander McCall-Smith, and many more expanded my interest in the countries of Africa. I read about places like the Mountains of the Moon and the Serengeti Plain, and let delightful words like Tanganyika, Zanzibar, and Zambezi roll off my tongue. In retrospect, it was inevitable that I would make it to the African continent someday.

Mike and I have been on seven safaris so far. We've visited Kenya, Tanzania, and Uganda in East Africa and the southern African countries of Botswana, Zambia, Zimbabwe, and South Africa. We both find it exhilarating to spend our days in the open air on safari vehicles or boats, watching animals hunt, play, fight, and otherwise live their lives. In most national parks or animal reserves, the animals are habituated to the presence of safari vehicles. They see the SUV and its occupants as one large entity and ignore us for the most part. However, anytime people step out of the vehicle, the animals see us as fair game.

There's a lovely rhythm to a safari that envelopes travelers. I find, much more than with most vacations, that rhythm immerses me in the present, in the beauty and pace of the wild. Depending upon the country and choice of safaris, visitors can spend hours or even entire days traveling from one national park or wildlife reserve to the next by safari vehicle or small plane. But when travelers arrive at their safari destination, the days are full. Animals are active in the early morning and late afternoon/early evening, so the daily schedule aligns with the animals' daily patterns. Rising before dawn for a morning game drive, safari guests usually head out of camp just as the sun rises. In the late morning, they usually return to camp for food and rest. Then, in the late afternoon, they're back out in the bush until sunset. Guests arrive in camp or their lodge for dinner, then go to bed, exhausted from the fresh air only to start again the next morning at dawn.

Sometimes, we've spent the entire day out on game drives, especially when our destination lay far from camp. At Kalahari Plains Camp in southern Botswana, we took a full day to explore the starkly beautiful Desolation Valley. We stopped at midday in a grove of trees where staff from Kalahari Plains had set up a tasty alfresco lunch. The animal highlight of the day came when we spotted several cheetahs. One allowed our vehicle to approach quite near.

In Tanzania, the Ngorongoro Crater, an extinct volcano thick with wildlife, operates on a daily permit system. Trips into the crater are all-day trips as well. We've visited the crater several times, with each journey revealing new animal sightings and exciting highlights. One time, we saw a mama rhino and her baby. Another time, we watched a herd of Cape buffalo battle a trio of lions on the hunt. The buffalo won, chasing the male of the pride into a ravine where he took cover. On our initial visit, we got our first real close-up of a leopard, which completely ignored our presence as he lounged on a fallen tree trunk in a secluded grove of trees.

One of my favorite safari activities is a night game drive. Some parks/ reserves allow night drives. Others don't. But it's a unique experience to proceed through the bush in the dark without headlights, guided only by a handheld beacon while trying to spot animals. Guides use a red filter over the light so as not to impair the animals' night vision. After sunset, many predators go on the prowl. Prides of lions and clans of hyenas travel long distances on their hunts. Impala and other herd animals huddle together, alert for danger. But the most fun is finding the animals that you can only see at night. Tiny, saucer-eyed bush babies scamper through the shrubs. Spring hares hop out of their burrows. Smaller nocturnal animals like servals and civets slink through the underbrush. In the black of night, these animals, large and small, can only be spotted by the flash of their eyes in the red light.

Safaris are not all about the animals. An inescapable aspect of every safari we've taken has been the food—almost always good with so many opportunities to sample it. Most of the safari camps serve primarily American, British, and European travelers, so I have always found many familiar dishes. However, both lodges and camps offer special nights with local cuisine, often served in an outdoor setting like a Boma (a replica of the wooden structures local tribes use to protect their livestock from predators).

Most of our days in camp started with tea or coffee and biscuits delivered to our tent or served in the main dining hall. After a couple of hours on a game drive, the guide stopped, whether traveling by vehicle or boat, and served more tea/coffee and breakfast snacks at a scenic spot in the bush. When we arrived back in camp around ten or eleven in the morning, we enjoyed a substantial brunch or lunch. Right before we left for the afternoon game drive, tea was available. Not just tea, the drink. An English tea with beverage, hors d'oeuvres like samosas or tiny sand-wiches, and cake or other sweets. On the afternoon game drive, the guide stopped for sundowners at sunset, usually offering our preferred alcoholic or nonalcoholic beverages and snacks. And, upon return to camp, we had time for drinks at the bar or in our tent, then dinner. Depending upon the camp, evening meals were buffet-style or served at our table. Seating ranged from private tables to a group table with all guests.

Some camps make a concerted effort to offer magical experiences in the bush, like the Desolation Valley lunch. Often, they stage special happy hours arranged by camp staff at breathtaking locations. In Samburu National Park in Kenya, we had sundowners on the top of a small hill and watched a glorious sunset descend beyond several tall acacia trees. At Botswana's Tubu Tree, we munched canapés as we watched herds of elephants take dust baths, silhouetted against the setting sun. At Toka Leya in Zambia, our guide docked our boat at an overlook where we sat on camp chairs to watch the sun drop into the mighty Zambezi River. And, at Vumbura Plains in Botswana, our guide spirited us away to a dinner out in the wild where staff had set up tables and served us a full-course meal complete with china and white tablecloths. As we dined, we were serenaded by the sounds of the savanna at night and enough decorative mason jar solar lights to suggest a fairyland.

Mike and I prefer tented camps, although we've also stayed in lodges. While we've bedded down in some basic tents in mobile camps, most tented camps are light-years from "roughing it." The tents and other more architecturally complex tented structures come fully furnished with beds, chests, chairs, even couches. All have bathrooms within the tent's structure. Most have showers, some outdoors with a view. A few have bathtubs as well.

Although I enjoy luxury in the bath, I've had the most fun bathing in the more rustic mobile camps where staff heat the water on an open fire and pour the water into an external tank for a hot shower. I enjoy the challenge of trying to finish my shower without the warm water running out, especially if washing my hair. Equally invigorating is taking an outdoor shower in an elevated tent while watching elephants and zebra wander by the "open wall" to the plain or river out front. The companies that design these tented camps do a masterful job of assuring privacy while giving guests a sense of immersion in the wild.

Whether in lodges or tents, most rooms have expansive windows to provide access to a bush view with its ever-changing parade of animals and birds. The décor skews heavily toward rustic safari with emphasis on local handicrafts and animal photography. Some, like the iconic Jack's Camp in the Makgadikgadi Salt Pans of Botswana, transport guests to the past with an *Out of Africa* vibe and lanternlight in the tents. I understand that Jack's has recently upgraded their tents. I hope they've maintained the same ambiance.

We've stayed in a wide variety of other accommodations, from very basic canvas tents or cabins to modern wooden suites or inns with a colonial manor house feel. Nearly every safari accommodation we've sampled has been situated in an amazing scenic location. Even the large lodges that perch on Tanzania's Ngorongoro Crater rim make up for their mass-tourism feel with spectacular views of the crater floor. Watching tendrils of mist from the highlands slither silently over the volcano rim like Ringwraiths on the hunt sets the perfect tone for a day of adventure among the dense concentration of animals at the bottom of the steep slope.

Many tented camps are elevated, with boardwalks leading from the main dining tent to the guest tents. We've stayed at others with ground-level boardwalks and, at several mobile camps that shift location with animal migrations or seasons, on the ground with just dirt paths. In all these tented camps and even most of the lodges, guests can walk the boardwalks or paths during the daylight hours on their own. After dark, guides must accompany guests to and from their rooms because of the wild animals.

In these camps, we quickly learned that we were in the animals' territory. In Mombo Camp, a high-end camp in Botswana with elevated boardwalks, we were cautioned not to run on the walks, especially at night, because the leopards that sometimes wander into camp would view a running human as prey. Brushing my teeth one morning at Mombo, I watched and listened to a herd of Cape buffalo mill around underneath our tent, their snorting and rumbling disturbing the quiet of breaking dawn. The camp's small plunge pool often filled with baboons taking a dip, something that discouraged me from afternoon swims.

At another camp in Botswana, Savuti, our escort had to find a roundabout way back to our tent after dinner one night because a small herd of elephants was systematically tearing up the boardwalk. Elephants are the largest creatures in Africa, and they like to stick to established paths or sometimes just don't like taking a detour to their destination. Given that they have the strength to tear down obstacles in their way, they can wreak havoc on camp boardwalk systems. This night, even after we had safely entered our room, one of the elephants kept rubbing up against one of the outer canvas walls as she finished trashing the boardwalk leading to our tent. Many of the camps now construct breaks in their walkway systems that allow elephants and other big animals to stroll through, thus avoiding the need to rebuild toppled handrails time and time again.

A simply outstanding camp in Kenya, Governor's Camp, takes an old-school approach. The tents all rest at ground level at its site on the Mara River. At dinner, we would watch hippos lumber up the bank from the river and walk right through the grounds on their way to feed. Since hippos are dangerous to encounter, whether on land or in water, camp guards stood watch all night to ensure guests returning to their tents didn't stumble across hippos marching to and from the water. Other animals, such as giraffes, often ambled through during the day. We had a trio of warthogs that hung out near our tent, but they just scurried away whenever they saw us.

Although every camp and guide emphasized time and again not to leave our tent at night, we received a compelling lesson in why during our first safari to Tanzania. We were staying in a mobile tented camp in a remote area of the Serengeti Plain. On the return from the first afternoon's game drive, we stopped to observe a leopard in a tree less than a mile from camp. That night, I awoke when an animal rustled by the tent, brushing the canvas next to my cot with a low rumbling growl as it passed. I spent the next hour lying awake in the dark, worried that the big cat would burst through the front flap of the tent—an irrational fear since we'd zipped the tent up tight. But I'd never had a lethal cat ripple the canvas wall touching my bed before! Eventually, I fell asleep, still uneaten. The following day, guides confirmed from the animal's sounds and the footprints in camp that a leopard had passed through. Lesson learned: Stay inside the tent at night.

Of course, like at Governor's Camp, animals don't always wait until sundown to frequent these tented camps or other accommodations in the wild. At a big lodge on the edge of Tanzania's Ngorongoro Crater, Mike and I were relaxing on our ground-floor balcony late one afternoon when a herd of elephants shuffled one by one down a narrow pathway just a few feet from us. We could smell the dusty, musky smell of elephant as they passed.

At Little Makalolo Camp in Hwange National Park in Zimbabwe, elephants would stroll right through camp day and night on their way to the water hole a few hundred yards away. The plus side of the elephant traffic was that the camp had a wooden blind where we took stellar close-up photos of the great beasts.

Farther north in Zimbabwe at Little Ruchomechi, which sits on the bank of the Zambezi River near Mana Pools, Mike and I were trapped in our tent for half an hour one day. A group of feisty elephants decided to feast on the trees near our cabin. At a rustic camp on the Linyanti River in Botswana, we lounged on our bed one afternoon and watched a mama and baby kudu munch leaves from the bush that bordered our front porch. A herd of zebra hung out around the dining hall most days at a remote tented camp on the Serengeti in Tanzania. They became part of the routine when we walked to meals, cantering away at the last moment as we neared.

A major downside to living amongst wild animals is that the African bush is not the place to just go for a stroll. So, a safari tends to become somewhat sedentary, with most of the time spent riding in vehicles or boats. I try to convince myself that all the bouncing around on bad dirt roads, and sometimes, off-road through high grass, over trees, and more, is a form of workout. And, in most camps, the tents are spread out over long distances, which require a good bit of walking. So, those activities provide moderate exercise.

Plus, we've had opportunities for some limited walking in the bush on most of our safaris. At Jack's Camp in Botswana, we climbed down from the vehicle and interacted with a habituated meerkat colony. Many people are familiar with this species from the popular Animal Planet TV show *Meerkat Manor*. These little animals were fun to observe up close. I sat on the ground as they scampered out of their underground burrows and stood upright, always alert for danger. They had no fear of Mike and me as they scurried around us and over our feet. The guide said that, sometimes, they would run right up onto your shoulder, trying to reach the highest elevation possible to search for predators. No such luck for me.

"Topping Off the Tanks" by Mike Knowlton. Little Makalolo Camp ...

...near Hwange National Park, Zimbabwe. 2014

We've twice gone on walks in a rhino preserve. Since poachers target these animals for their horns, this preserve has gathered a herd of rhinos in a protected space. The conservation organization helps subsidize the operation by taking visitors on walks to observe the animals. We were asked not to reveal the location or post photos with position tracking on social media, so I won't indicate where this took place. Rangers, armed with rifles, accompanied our small group on the walk over the savanna. These men and women guard the endangered animals day and night. Staying downwind from the herd, we were able to get quite close. But it was a little nerve-wracking to be on foot near such huge animals.

Another drawback to staying in camps in the African wild can be the monkeys, especially baboons and vervets.

I should preface these paragraphs with the caveat that my opinion of monkeys might be colored by my early experience with a friend's spider monkey. For several months, Willie lived just down the hall in my college dorm with two of my best friends. They often gave him the run of their room, and the little beast loved to jump on my head when I entered. He'd nip at my scalp and claw my hair, a treatment he reserved primarily for me. Let's just say our relationship was not the best. Eventually, the dorm authorities discovered the monkey and threw Willie out. It's not clear that the college ever contemplated monkeys when they wrote their no-pets-in-the-dorm policy. So, my friends got some credit for innovation, but the dorm authorities ruled No Monkeys. While my girlfriends were sad to see Willie go, I couldn't have been more thrilled to see the last of that little imp.

Many of Africa's primate species are much larger than Willie. Baboons, the world's largest monkeys, can be bold, even savage. At an outdoor market near Victoria Falls one morning, we watched several baboons wait in the trees in the parking lot, then swoop down to steal items right out of shoppers' hands. We saw one big guy rip a Coke out of a man's hand and swing back up in the tree to enjoy his booty. We've also seen baboons terrorizing unsuspecting tourists for snacks or shiny objects at many border checkpoints or park offices. I always take a very wary view of these sharp-toothed creatures and steer clear.

Our most exasperating baboon experience occurred at a Botswana camp called Chitabe, where the large canvas tents nestled under a stand of mature trees. One afternoon, Mike and I were trying to nap during the post-lunch rest period when wham! Something thudded onto the tent roof and slid from the peak to the edge. Something large. Soon, lots of heavy things began to drop onto the peak and slide to the edge of the canopy. When I looked out the screened side window, I found an upside-down pair of baboon eyes staring in at us. And, so, afternoon playtime for the baboons began. They were using the roof of our tent just like kids use the slides at a playground.

Mike and I went outside and tried to chase them away, but the baboons were having too much fun. Soon, attracted by all the commotion and screeching, people from the nearby tents wandered down to watch the show. Mike and I never got that nap. And my dislike of baboons became more personal.

Smaller monkeys, like vervets, certainly are cuter than baboons. But they can be destructive too. As monkey prevention, most camps instruct guests, "Always zip up your tents or latch your doors." At lodging with a large resident monkey population, the precautions are usually more robust. For example, at Mara Intrepids Camp in Kenya, the vervets had already mastered opening zippers, so padlocks augmented the tent zippers. We were told to keep them always locked and to store no food in our tents. We found out why when the woman in the tent next door broke protocol. She'd failed to completely zip her tent shut, let alone use the padlock. When she came out of the shower one afternoon, a tent full of rambunctious monkeys greeted her; the screaming first alerted us.

Camp management arrived, shooed out the monkeys, and calmed our fellow traveler. The next day, she zipped her tent but still didn't engage the padlock. Even more foolish, she left a bag of chocolate out on an end-table. When she went on a game drive, monkeys struck again—a great lesson on the wisdom of following the rules when it comes to monkeys.

But Mike and I discovered that, sometimes, even following the rules couldn't protect us. At a camp perched on a rocky outcrop near Lake Mburo in Uganda, we stayed in a small stucco cottage with a wooden front door and screened windows. The managers cautioned us about monkeys and warned against keeping food in our rooms. We watched several vervets race through the open-air dining area at breakfast the first morning and snatch bananas off the buffet table, despite two staff people standing monkey guard.

When Mike and I returned from our game drive the next morning, the camp manager met us with a glum look on her face. While we were away, monkeys had pried the screen from the stucco wall and raided our cottage. What a mess. It looked like a small tornado had hit the room. The creatures had rifled through our toiletries, chewed our toothbrushes and toothpaste. Tossed some of our clothes around. Worst of all, one of the nasty little fellows had defecated on my backpack. His buddies stole two bottles of Mike's medication.

The camp gave us new toothbrushes and toothpaste. We threw several other toiletry items away. I gritted my teeth and cleaned up the backpack. But the one thing we couldn't replace out in the middle of the Ugandan wild was Mike's medicine. Desperate, he followed a trail of pills onto the nearby rocks outside our cottage. Like Sherlock Holmes pursuing a case, he picked up many tablets from the ground while a group of vervets, probably the very marauders that trashed our room, chattered at him from the trees. Fortunately, he could retrieve most of the pills, but some of the monkeys' blood pressure may have dropped to dangerously low levels. I've enjoyed almost every camp where we've stayed in Africa, but I must admit that I will try to avoid camps with pillaging monkeys.

Not all our small primate experiences have been unpleasant. Watching various monkey species scamper through the trees, including mothers with babies clinging to their backs, can be amusing. I love encountering Colobus monkeys with their striking long black-and-white fur as they perch on high branches. And our hike into the jungle to find a chimpanzee colony at Kibale in Uganda was a once-in-a-lifetime experience. We spent several hours watching the chimps going about their lives in the forest canopy far above our heads.

The good and the bad are all part of the African safari experience. And, for me, the adventure far outweighs any inconvenience, even from a band of thieving monkeys. Watching the sunrise over a plain thick with wildebeest and zebra; sitting by the campfire and thrilling to a lion roar in the night; hearing the crystalline tinkle of bell frogs at dusk; seeing the elemental life-and-death struggle of predator and prey unfold in real-time—all these things, large and small, make the African bush one of my favorite places on Earth.

I would be remiss not to make one thing clear. Mike and I have visited enough tribal villages and slums of cities like Nairobi and Johannesburg to understand that a safari is not the reality of life for millions who live on the African continent. Many Africans live in poverty. Others work backbreaking jobs in the oilfields or diamond mines. Still more make barely a subsistence living as cattle herders, farmers, or fishers. Some countries' political situations are unstable or worse. Periodic waves of terrorism and modern tribal warfare resurface time and again in pockets across the continent.

A sad fact is that many citizens of those countries that attract safari enthusiasts like Mike and me have never seen the iconic animals that bring foreigners flocking to their parks and reserves. Many of the most socially conscious safari companies are trying to expand the citizenry's connection with the wild animals that are both their countries' legacy and a valuable economic resource. Safari companies train and employ locals as guides, camp managers, and camp staff. In some areas, native tribes own the land and run the safari operations. We've stayed at several Maasai-owned camps. Other operators work with schools and village elders to bring children into the parks to develop an appreciation for the animals. I've been pleased to encounter busloads of school kids on educational trips to national parks in Kenya and Tanzania.

Since our interest is primarily the animals, Mike and I have not yet traveled to African countries that don't offer safaris or are too unstable to visit. Africa is a vast continent, more than three times larger in landmass than the United States. Here in the States, we often talk about Africa as one monolithic place and think of the continent as filled with the type of wild animals that Tarzan saw when swinging through the jungle canopy.

In fact, there are fifty-four countries in Africa that include tourist meccas with mostly desert topography like Morocco, oil-rich Nigeria, war-torn countries like the Democratic Republic of the Congo and Somalia, and South Africa with its cosmopolitan cities like Cape Town and Johannesburg. Like North America, the continent is very diverse with cities, towns, and rural and wild areas that differ widely in their economies, focus, and the kind of life each offers.

Mike and I are already planning our next trip to Africa. While the continent has much variety to offer travelers, we'll return primarily for the safari experience that we love. We'd like to visit some new-to-us countries like Namibia and Rwanda. Not long ago, I wrote a love letter to southern Africa in the form of a novel. The book, a volume in the suspense series I author, was released in 2021. *Dead on the Delta* takes place primarily in Botswana. In the months I spent writing the book, each word I typed made me want to return once more to the Okavango Delta. So, it's likely we'll also go back to Botswana. As I said, Africa has gotten into my blood.

9

Indiana Jones Moments

WHEN I think of travel adventures, Indiana Jones movies usually leap to mind. Yes, Indy is usually fighting Nazis and other villains. But his escapades take him to ancient temples, high mountains, crowded bazaars, and other colorful spots all over the globe. The entire Indiana Jones series provides a cultural smorgasbord for its audience. In addition to the exotic locales, unexpected adventure and Indy's ability to meet challenges head-on are the other hallmarks of the movies. Although much of our travel takes us into unfamiliar and fascinating territory, I confess, Mike and I have never had to fight Nazis or escape from foreign thugs. However, similar, perhaps less-cinematic experiences have made our travel special too.

I'm drawn to ancient structures that may be worn or crumbling but have survived centuries and can still capture the imagination of a modern traveler. One of those places is Borobudur, a Buddhist stupa temple on the island of Java in Indonesia. Our small group of ten started a hike to the temple in the predawn hours from a hotel at the foot of the mountain. Out of respect for religious traditions, we wore black and white sarongs knotted around our waists as we walked. After stumbling through the dark on a rocky trail, our path lit only by the wavering beams of our flashlights, we faced a long flight of stairs to the top level of the temple.

Borobudur, built in the ninth century, is the world's largest Buddhist temple. The temple consists of nine stacked platforms, six square and three circular, topped by a central dome. In all, it rises 95-feet tall. Made of native stone set without mortar, the temple incorporates 2,672 carved

"Monk, U Bein Bridge" by Sherry Knowlton. Taungthaman Lake, Myanmar. 2014

panels and 504 Buddha statues. Seventy-two Buddha statues, each seated inside a perforated dome-shaped stupa, surround the central dome.[4]

We reached the top of the hill, still in the dark. By the time we'd climbed to the upper level of the temple, dawn was breaking. We quickly secured seats on the temple stones in time to watch the sun rise over twin volcanoes in the distance, Mount Merbabu and Mount Merapi. To contemplate that humans have sat in the same place and watched the sun rise over those two volcanoes for more than twelve centuries gave the entire experience a unique level of significance. When I look at our photos from Borobudur or just think back upon that morning, I always smile and feel calm radiate through my body.

I felt a similar sense of awe at U Bein bridge in Mandalay, Myanmar, this time as I watched the sun set. Perhaps there's something about witnessing these daily sun cycles that inspires reflection. U Bein, which spans Taungthaman Lake, is considered the oldest teak bridge in the world. Still an important passageway for locals, the bridge has also become a tourist attraction for both its history and the compelling silhouette the raised structure presents against the setting sun. The night we visited U Bein, I watched a perfect sunset dip behind the sturdy yet elegant structure and captured a great photograph of a robed Buddhist monk walking the bridge. The design is much newer than Borobudur, having reached completion in 1851. However, the monk, the hand-built quality of the bridge, and the endurance of this wooden feat of engineering made me feel I'd glimpsed something both exotic and special.

A different kind of Indiana Jones-style adventure involved another elephant ride. We rose at dawn one morning to search for tigers in Chitwan National Park in Nepal. But unlike the open jeeps of the Indian national parks, here we rode elephants, four of us in a basket on the big beast's back. A mahout sat on the elephant's neck to guide the animal.

The terrain of Chitwan near our camp was flat with a mix of hardwood forest and grasslands. Our party set out on two elephants in heavy ground fog, the mist so thick that our companions' elephant disappeared

---

4 UNESCO. "Borobudur Temple Compounds." Accessed November 16, 2021. https://whc.unesco.org/en/list/592/

from view when it walked just a few yards ahead. Then we plunged into elephant grass, looking for tigers. The elephants lumbered steadily through the damp grass, so tall it brushed the animals' shoulders. We searched the savanna for a glimpse of a tiger, but as we'd learned in India, it would be difficult to see a tiger in vegetation this dense, even if it was sitting just a few feet away. Nor did any emerge into the rare open breaks among the grasses.

The mist lifted as the day warmed, but after several hours, we'd found no tigers. Not long after the mahouts left the grasslands and entered the forest, we saw the leopard. The camp guide had told us that while Chitwan included leopards on its list of native species, they were infrequent. But there, right in front of us, was a beautiful leopard sprawled across the nearly horizontal limb of a tall tree. The mahouts commanded the elephants forward until we stopped about ten feet away from the tree. That's when it registered that the tree branch wasn't quite so high when viewed from our perch on the back of a nine-foot-tall elephant. We sat just a few feet below leopard eye level.

I spied the dead deer in a crook of the limb just as the leopard began to growl a warning. The elephants, spooked by the yowling cat, the smell of blood, or maybe both, started to shuffle. They protested with a loud rumbling from deep in their throats, the sounds building as the two elephants' distress fed off each other.

Meanwhile, Mike snapped photo after photo of the snarling leopard with dazzling blue eyes. I also watched the leopard but kept a hand on the rim of our basket seat in case our elephant decided to bolt.

Finally, the guide asked the mahouts, who'd been trying to calm their respective elephants, to back away from the tree. We gave the leopard considerable space before we halted again. The big cat relaxed a bit but clearly had no intention of leaving its breakfast. When we finally began the trek back to camp, both elephants had calmed enough for an uneventful return trip.

Although we hadn't seen a tiger, the leopard sighting more than compensated. Blown away that we'd seen a leopard, our guide and camp staff admitted that they'd seen none in the area for over a year. What an adventure.

Another unique experience that sticks with me took place much closer to home in the US Capitol in Washington, DC. We have a long-time friend who served in senior staff positions on various committees in Congress throughout his career. In the late 1980s, we were visiting for the weekend when he had to pick up some paperwork from his office. He invited us to go along and offered an after-hours tour of the Capitol. Although both Mike and I had been to the Capitol building, we jumped at the offer. So, our friend, his wife, Mike, and I took a private tour of key public spaces of our nation's almost-deserted Capitol building. We did see some Capitol police when our friend signed us in, but mostly we slipped through the dimly lit and hushed corridors like wraiths. The highlight came in the shadowy Hall of Statues, where our friend showed us the whispering trick made possible by the acoustics of the Capitol dome. One can stand in the rotunda at certain spots and be heard clearly many yards away. Similar demonstrations of this whispering effect have become part of most Capitol tours. However, the solitude of the huge Capitol and the silence in the unlit dome made the experience uniquely eerie. Just the three of us standing in the dark and hearing our friend, lost in the shadows behind a statue, whisper a few lines from the preamble to the Declaration of Independence.

The sad footnote to this experience is that it's unlikely it could happen today. Post-9/11, security restrictions for the Capitol make it harder for the public to obtain after-hours access to the seat of our government. Between the COVID-19 pandemic and the 2021 insurrection at the Capitol building, few people beyond government officials are even permitted in the building today.

Another place that had me channeling Indiana was at the hanging bridges of Arenal in Costa Rica. This park features a series of wooden slatted bridges strung throughout the rainforest canopy. Walking among the lush trees at bird's-eye level offered a unique perspective on the thick rainforest below. Although uncrowded when we visited, Arenal is a popular stop in tours of Costa Rica. My feeling of adventure stemmed more from a personal sense of accomplishment. I am afraid of heights, so I was wary about whether I'd be able to walk these bridges, especially the tallest at 148 feet above the ground. But I did. I powered through my fears and finished the entire two-mile series of trails and canopy bridges—although I suffered a few heart-stopping moments in the middle when the longest bridge started to vibrate and sway from my footsteps.

In fact, the Arenal experience bolstered my courage enough to later brave the Capilano Suspension Bridge and Treetops Park outside Vancouver, British Columbia. There, I made it across the suspension bridge that spans the Capilano River, which is much higher at 230 feet. After crossing the big daddy, the wooden network of shorter bridges nestled among the towering evergreens in the rest of the walk held few terrors. However, I did take a pass on the Cliff Walk, a cantilevered curved walkway that juts out into thin air over the canyon. After all, even the intrepid Indiana Jones feared snakes!

In one of our early trips to Tanzania, Mike, Josh, his girlfriend at the time, and I visited a Hadzabe bushman camp in Tanzania. This nomadic tribe follows wild game and the seasons; their temporary huts were small structures of woven branches and grasses. Our main activity with the tribe involved accompanying the chief's son on a hunt for giraffe. The bushmen were armed with bow and poison-tipped arrows as they struck out into the sandy wild with our small group trailing along. We followed the lead warrior down a dry riverbed until he climbed up the bank and struck out into a scrub forest. Josh kept pace with the bushman, but the rest of us fell behind and continued to meander down the riverbed when we lost track of the bushman and my son. Two younger tribesmen appeared, probably to keep an eye on the clueless tourists, so we didn't become completely lost. At one point, Mike, Josh's girlfriend, and I looked at each other and said, "Where the heck are we?" We were all a little uneasy but kept walking.

Then, the topography changed, and we arrived at the top of a sandy ridge. Below, there was a small lake. A large party of brightly dressed travelers had dismounted to water their camels and looked like they were setting up camp for the night. For a moment, it seemed like we'd walked through a crack in the globe and stepped from Tanzania into the Middle

East. Then, the young bushmen motioned for us to turn around and follow them. The road back, as always, seemed shorter than our original exploration into strange territory. After about half an hour, we met up with Josh and his now-buddy bushman. Although Josh later told us that he'd had a blast dashing through the scrub forest with the bushman on the hunt, they hadn't bagged a giraffe.

Upon our return to camp, we met the warrior's new bride and baby as well as his father, the tribe's chief. Some of our group joined the tribe in an archery competition (with poison-free arrows) and dances. Much later, only after we'd driven away from the tribe, did it fully hit me that we'd spent an entire afternoon wandering around the wilds of Tanzania, virtually on our own. Josh had disappeared for about an hour along with the guy we were supposed to be following. Our guide had stayed back in camp, and no one in our group could communicate with the two young boys who spoke only that unique click-based language used by bushmen. Foolish or adventurous? Perhaps a little of both, but it's a memory that stays with me to this day as a lot of fun.

Our best ancient architecture adventure unfolded in Mexico. Mike, Josh, and I were staying in Tulum, at that time a small, sleepy village on the Yucatán coast. I understand that the area has become a jet-set haven and, recently, a dangerous spot in Mexico's drug wars. So, I'm glad we visited when it was relatively unspoiled. Tulum itself has an impressive Mayan ruin, made even more striking because it's perched on the edge of the ocean. We visited the seaside ruins soon after we arrived, but even in the late 1990s, the site was filled with tourists on day trips from Cancún and elsewhere on the Riviera Maya.

We'd heard about another Mayan ruin about an hour inland. So, one morning, we drove our Jeep over narrow and isolated country roads to Coba for what became a total Indiana Jones experience. At that time, archeologists had excavated most of Coba from the jungle, although a few structures in the large complex were still being unearthed. We pulled into the gravel parking lot, empty but for a single car. A snoozing man in the ticket booth woke up long enough to collect our small payment, hand us a crude map, and tell us to "just follow the path."

The three of us walked the dirt path through the jungle for ten or fifteen minutes without seeing another soul. Suddenly, the trail ended, and there before us rose a towering Mayan pyramid, Nohoch Mul, looming gray and formidable against a vast tropical jungle. So, we climbed it. Even today, Coba permits tourists to climb this and some of the other ancient structures.

We took our time mounting the 130 steps to the top of the pyramid. An attached rope helped us navigate the steep climb. Standing on the top was an exhilarating experience. At 137 feet in the air, we stood above the jungle canopy, a sea of green stretching in all directions. I could believe, for a moment, that we'd left the modern world and entered the world of the first-century Mayans who'd built Coba. It was just the Knowlton family, no other humans in the vicinity, standing on the precipice of a primeval jungle. What an intoxicating feeling.

However, what goes up must come down. After a long rest on the top of the pyramid, we had to make our way back to earth. The descent also turned into another breathtaking experience, but not in a good way. I have a lifelong fear, not of heights, per se, but of heights with edges. The thrill of standing on the broad top of the pyramid had been enough to repress any anxiety. But the only way down was those same steep stone steps, and this time I had to face forward. I feel no shame in confessing that I descended on my rear, sliding step by step by step until I reached a point close enough to the ground that I felt comfortable finishing upright.

Was the terror of my clamber back down Nohoch Mul worth it? Absolutely. I can only describe the thrill and the view from the pinnacle of the ancient pyramid as priceless. We spent several more hours that day wandering through the mysterious ruins, many of them covered in moss and vines. At its height of glory between 200 and 600 AD, Coba was among the largest Mayan cities with 50,000 residents. The other ruins include a stone road system, a ball court, and slabs containing glyphs and drawings that provide a lasting record of what daily Mayan life was like. We saw only two other sets of visitors and a groundskeeper on a bicycle during that entire day.

I love that I've had the opportunity to experience Indiana Jones-worthy moments in my travels. Greeting the sunrise at Java's ancient

Borobudur. Watching a lone monk tread the worn boards of Myanmar's U Bein bridge. Slipping through the deserted corridors of the US Capitol in the still of the night surrounded by the ghosts of our nation's forefathers. Navigating a treetop bridge in the Costa Rican rainforest. Standing on the top of a Mayan pyramid in a Yucatán jungle. Enthusiasm for new places and new experiences combined with preparation for the unexpected and a pinch of courage make sensational Indiana Jones moments possible for any traveler.

'Lion Interrupted' by Mike Knowlton. Serengeti Plain, Tanzania. 2017

Close Encounters of the Scary Kind

TRAVELING AS much as Mike and I do, we've inevitably run into occasional problems or experienced close calls. However, going back to our hiking days and that "Be Prepared" motto, we plan our itineraries to avoid problems. Sometimes, that means we're not as spontaneous as we'd like. Other times we might pass on a destination or must change our plans.

In 1990, we were well into the planning stage with some friends for a trip to Turkey. The centerpiece of the trip was to be a week on a *gulet* in the Mediterranean. A cruise on one of these small traditional sailing boats had been on my to-do list for years. But then the Gulf War erupted, and we decided that the entire region was too uncertain for a trip to Turkey. Decades later, we've not yet managed to visit there.

Disease outbreaks also have caused us to cancel trips. We were just a few months away from leaving for a trip to Brazil's Pantanal to look for jaguars in the wild when Zika emerged as a new concern. In the early stages, rural Brazil was hit particularly hard with the illness, so we canceled even though we didn't fit the primary at-risk category. Medical experts knew too little about Zika at that time for us to take a chance.

More recently, the COVID-19 pandemic forced us to postpone a trip to England, Ireland, and Scotland. Quarantines, travel restrictions, and the lack of a vaccine or cure for the disease in summer 2020 made the decision to delay an easy one. With each of these changes in plans, we had regrets about canceling an anticipated trip. But the adage "better safe than sorry" applies to elective travel. It's one thing if something unexpected happens mid-trip. It's another to knowingly take a foolish risk.

Other times, we've embarked on a trip, and, despite the most flawless itinerary, something goes wrong. Sometimes a broad issue affects an entire area, like the labor strikes that shut down parts of Paris one week. We simply worked around the strikes and found unaffected places in the city to spend our days. Other times, an unforeseen development has impacted our fellow travelers and us much more directly. We've never experienced anything that disrupted an entire trip or caused us lasting bodily harm. But we have had several close calls.

One of our most traumatic disruptions occurred on the Alaska Star Railroad during a return trip from Denali National Park. Mike and I were seated four cars back from the engine, so when the train made an abrupt stop, we jerked a bit in our seats but were more surprised than alarmed.

Soon, however, we learned the reason for the unexpected halt. The train had hit a pick-up truck on the tracks, killing the driver. The impact from the emergency stop left a few of our fellow passengers in the first train car with bumps and bruises, but Mike and I were okay. From the outdoor platform of our car, we could catch a glimpse of the mangled pick-up truck as we waited for police and ambulances. No one could have survived the collision.

Because of Federal regulations, the police had to call in the National Transportation and Safety Board (NTSB). So, we waited. The train sat on the tracks for more than five hours while the authorities carried out their investigation. Finally, the NTSB gave the railroad the okay to use the second engine to push the passenger cars back a few miles to a road crossing. We never learned if the first engine was damaged and unable to move or impounded as part of the accident review. However, it never moved while we remained at the crash scene.

The sun had set before we and the hundreds of other stranded passengers loaded onto the buses that arrived. We stumbled into our Anchorage hotel close to midnight, following an almost two-hour ride on dark, narrow roads. Barely sleeping during a short, restless night, we soon rose to catch a very early flight to Juneau to join our small boat cruise.

Although this accident didn't affect us personally, it was a sobering experience, especially during a carefree vacation. As we spent hours waiting on the tracks, passengers and crew speculated about how such an accident could have happened. The afternoon was bright and sunny. This remote railroad crossing had no crossbar but was equipped with working flashing lights. The vehicle driver would have had a clear, unobstructed view of the track and oncoming train as well as ample auditory warning. The engineer had sounded his horn in advance of this crossing as he had at all the others.

Word began to spread in the train, which news reports later confirmed. A woman had driven onto the tracks and stopped. She had died of suicide-by-train. We never learned more about the woman's situation or motivation but now know that Alaska has the highest per capita rate of suicide in the United States, with a rate almost double the national average. The train incident gave us a different perspective on the wild, lonely beauty of our northernmost state, especially when coupled with the refrain that we heard from so many Alaska residents we spoke to—that they lived there during the daylit summer but fled elsewhere to escape the long, dark winters that bring only a few hours of light each day. The amount of daylight varies depending on latitude, but many residents succumb to the lack of light, isolation, and other issues.

We've also confronted less-deadly transportation mishaps. Flat tires are ubiquitous on African safaris, and we've experienced quite a few. In some cases, bad roads and driving cross-country can lead to frequent punctures, even in a heavy-duty, designed-for-rough-terrain vehicle. Most of the time, our guides just found a place to pull over, unloaded all the passengers from the safari vehicle, and changed the tires, usually with Mike and one or two others helping.

However, when that flat happens at dusk just a few yards from a pride of lions, changing a tire can take on a whole new element of danger. That's precisely what happened to us once in Botswana. Mike and I were with two other couples. We'd just spent almost an hour watching a big lion pride that was hanging out in a brushy area beneath several large trees. The five adult females and two large males spent most of their time lounging. However, we had a great time watching three toddler-age cubs cavort on a huge fallen tree trunk, scampering along the trunk, slipping to the ground, and then jumping up to start the game all over again.

As the sun sank above the treetops, our guide, George, said, "We need to get back to camp."

He drove only a few minutes before the vehicle lurched. Flat tire. He hustled us out of the SUV to lessen the weight and said to the women, "Stand on the far side of the vehicle away from the lion pride. Stay alert for animals."

We could no longer see them but knew that lions rise from their daytime torpor to hunt at night. And, from a how-fast-can-a-pride-of-hungry-lions-travel-in-just-minutes perspective, we were well within the danger zone. What really brought that home was how nervous George seemed about the tire change. Sweat bathed his face before he even touched the tire jack. He asked Mike and another man to stand watch on his side of the vehicle, the one closest to the lions. The third male passenger helped with the work.

Night had fallen by the time the men had bolted the new tire in place. After spending twenty minutes on full alert, jumping at every rustle in the bush, we were relieved to head back to camp unscathed.

We've also experienced close calls in the air while in Africa. As I mentioned earlier, I love flying in small planes. But we've twice had problems with them. The first time occurred on a landing in Nairobi. Instead of the main international airport, smaller planes use a dedicated airfield, Wilson Airport, which has no control tower. After a smooth flight in from the remote Masai Mara plains, things got dicey very quickly. As our pilot descended for touchdown, another small plane taking off flew almost directly into our path. The pilots managed to make quick adjustments to avoid each other by what seemed like only a few feet. Ours later told us the gap was at least twenty yards, not as near a crash as I'd imagined but too close for safety. My heart still pounded when we disembarked. We flew out of Wilson at least two other times after that with no incident.

A less-dramatic landing took place on a flight to a camp near Hwange National Park in Zimbabwe. We flew in a tiny plane with just enough room for the pilot and our party of four Knowltons: Mike, Josh, Laura, and me. The camp runway was hard-packed but rough dirt; it felt like the plane was taxiing on a washboard after we landed.

We unloaded our bags, met our waiting guide, and stood by while the pilot climbed back into the plane for takeoff. However, the plane wouldn't start. After examining the engine, the pilot discovered that a critical part had broken, likely upon landing. Hard not to imagine what would have happened if the piece had malfunctioned in midair. Stranded, our pilot spent the night in camp and had to wait there until another plane flew in with a replacement part the next day. The same pilot and aircraft returned for us in four days. Thankfully, that flight landed with no problems.

Sometimes close calls can be avoided by staying informed, whether about a specific trip we're contemplating or about incidents that happen at a place we're thinking of visiting in the future. A picture of a riverboat in a travel brochure hooked Mike and me on the idea of a trip on Peru's Amazon River. Something about the sight of that small boat on the broad river beckoned. That photo declared, "This could be a great adventure."

As we researched the trip, however, we discovered that the boat in the brochure was one of three used by the company. And that, a year earlier, one of their boats sank during the night, causing its twenty-two passengers and almost as many crew members to flee in their nightclothes onto lifeboats in the dark river. Although no lives were lost, all the possessions, including passports, other papers, and money of the primarily American travelers sank with the boat. The travel agency and the embassies in Peru helped the affected travelers and arranged flights home, but what a terrible way to end a trip.

Alarm bells went off when we read about the riverboat sinking. Not the type of adventure we had in mind. We instantly had second thoughts. So, we did more research, read more recent traveler reviews, and contacted the travel company to discuss the incident. It turns out that the boat had been cruising at night on the Amazon during high water. A water-soaked log, floating unseen beneath the surface in the dark, had torn a hole in the hull below the waterline. It's not uncommon for entire trees to be swept into the river during the seasonal flood or for commercial boats transporting logs to lose some of their cargo.

A company vice-president assured me, "We immediately reevaluated our safety procedures after the accident. Our boats no longer travel at night. The crew now ties the boat up to a tree on the bank at sunset. We've had no more mishaps since instituting the revised procedures."

So, we decided to go for it and enjoyed our adventure, one without any damage to the boat. Even though our trip took place in a month with lower water levels, hefty trees did float by the boat from time to time. However, traveling in daylight, the captain could see them coming and avoid danger by changing course.

Learning about a much more tragic incident also made us think twice about taking a safari to Uganda. In planning our gorilla trek in the Bwindi Impenetrable Forest, we discovered that a large group of rebels had once attacked two Bwindi tourist camps, killing four Ugandan rangers and eight tourists, including an American couple. Bwindi is only a few miles from the Democratic Republic of the Congo (DRC) border and a short drive from Rwanda. The three countries share the mountainous habitat of the remaining one thousand endangered mountain gorillas. The attackers were ethnic Hutu rebels who'd fled Rwanda after the peace accord. At that time, chaos still reigned in the DRC, which had become a safe harbor for bandits and rebels.

Although the Bwindi tragedy gave us pause, this attack on the tourist camps had taken place in 1999, a decade before our trip. After further research, we concluded that there appeared to be little current danger, so we decided to proceed.

While in Uganda, one of our guides conveyed a sense of how difficult life can be in that volatile region of Africa. He'd served in the Ugandan army as a very young man during Joseph Kony's Lord's Resistance Army incursions into the country's northern region. Near the end of our two weeks with him, he felt comfortable enough to share some of his experience and even showed us his childhood home. Although years had passed since his stint in the army, much of the trauma of that experience simmered just below the amiable demeanor of a professional guide.

Research may also help alert travelers to the type of hazards that exist in a certain locale. But we've learned that being aware of the risks can't fully help us plan for natural disasters. We've been fortunate not to experience any devastating natural incidents. However, while staying in Queenstown, New Zealand, the region was hit by an earthquake. Coming from Pennsylvania, where our rare earthquakes are usually so small as to be imperceptible, I didn't realize what was happening at first. I was standing in our hotel bathroom, combing my hair, when all our family's toiletries just popped off the vanity onto the floor. I ran into the bedroom convinced that, somehow, my husband and son were playing a prank on me. Yes, I know how crazy this sounds. How could they have swept items from the bathroom counter when they were in another room? All I can say is, when confronted by the inexplicable, the mind always looks first for a familiar explanation.

"How did you do that?"

"Do what?" Mike asked, a startled look in his eyes.

"Knock everything off the bathroom counter," I persisted, even though I'd begun to glean from Mike's expression that he'd felt the big bump too.

Josh, an old New Zealand hand from his semester in Auckland, chuckled. "Mom. It was an earthquake."

"Earthquake?" Now, even more freaked out, I gasped, "Should we leave the hotel and get outside?"

"Nah," Josh replied. "The tremor seemed like a mild one."

From the news, we soon learned that the "mild" tremor was a magnitude seven earthquake, but the epicenter was in the ocean off Tasmania. So, the effect on the South Island, where we were staying, was relatively minor, as Josh had assessed, with no tsunami activity anticipated.

New Zealand sits on the trailing end of the volcanic region covering much of the South Pacific called the Ring of Fire. So, seismic activity in the country is not uncommon. During his semester at the University of Auckland, Josh experienced several earthquakes, none destructive. And, before this stop on the South Island, we'd visited Rotorua, New Zealand's version of Yellowstone, and had experienced its seismic activity, featuring a small area with geysers, steaming natural cauldrons, and hot springs.

We saw firsthand the more devastating consequences of living in the Pacific Ring of Fire when we later visited Java in Indonesia. Java is home to forty-five of Indonesia's one hundred and fifty volcanoes. One of Indonesia's most famous, Krakatoa, erupted in 1883 and discharged so much ash into the atmosphere that it affected the global climate.

Our guide took us to visit a Java village that a volcanic explosion had partially destroyed a few months before our arrival. Mount Merapi, one of the island's most active volcanoes, killed over 350 people in that eruption from both lava flow and noxious gasses. We could see lava trails and the remains of several destroyed homes and buildings. Sobering.

Several years later, another erupting volcano kept us on tenterhooks. We were just three days from flying to San Jose in Costa Rica when a nearby volcano, Turrialba, erupted. The eruption was relatively benign, with no injuries to anyone in the area. Because of the ash in the air, however, authorities closed the airport. We were relieved that the airfield opened the night before we flew in so we could begin our scheduled tour on time. However, we could see smoke still hovering over the volcano's cone as we landed.

Later in the trip, we spent a day near another Costa Rican volcano, Arenal. The prominent cone rises 5,436 feet into the air and is visible for miles. Sometimes, especially at night, visitors see "fireworks" from the volcano as it spits lava above the peak. However, the day we visited, only a cloud of smoke crowned the lush, green cone.

Although I did not join him, Mike hiked up the Soufrière Volcano on St. Vincent with his brother, Steve, and our sister-in-law, Pam, in 2018 when we stayed on the nearby Grenadine island of Bequia. They enlisted a guide for the steep and challenging trek to the rim of the volcano, which had been dormant for four decades. During the five-hour climb, they encountered no other hikers, just several locals who, according to the guide, likely worked in the marijuana fields hidden in the thick tropical jungle on the lower slopes of the volcano.

Imagine our shock when, just two years later, we read that the long-dormant Soufrière had erupted. Fortunately, Soufrière gave the seismologists enough warning that authorities could evacuate 20,000 people from the danger. The 2021 explosion harmed no one on St. Vincent. However, I suspect Mike will think twice before his next "dormant" volcano trek.

On a 2021 visit to Iceland, we passed on a tramp to see the active eruption of the Fagradalsfjall Volcano, even though the site had become quite a tourist destination. However, we did see the smoke from the erupting fissure from a distance.

I don't mind admitting that a very different type of natural disaster we faced—twice—had me sweating both times. Our first encounter with an African brush fire was at a remote camp called Tarangire Treetops near Tanzania's Tarangire National Park. The camp's wooden lodging, round rooms scattered over a small hillside, was built around trees two stories in the air. The property was located outside the national park on a seasonal road, more of a sandy track, that took almost forty-five minutes to navigate to reach a "main" road.

So, it was disconcerting when we came to the restaurant area for dinner on the third night of our stay and spotted a fire in the distance. A long, flickering orange line snaked from one side of the otherwise dark horizon to the other. When we expressed concern, camp staff reassured us in soothing voices: "Yes, it was a brushfire, but it remained on the other side of the riverbed. It had probably started from lightning igniting dry grasses, but the wind could have whipped flames out of control when a farmer was burning off crops."

When pressed, a manager assured us, "Not to worry, please. Some camp staff are out there helping to fight the fire. Soon they will stamp it out."

As we dined, we watched the flames burn closer and closer. While still a mile or two away, the danger was heading in our direction. At that time, Tanzania was in the grip of a long drought. On our way into Tarangire, we'd passed many carcasses of Maasai cattle, dead because there was so little water to sustain them. So, we knew that the dry brush and forest that stood between us and the fire would ignite in an instant as the flames crept forward.

The fire line still blazed in the distance when we returned to our room. The elevation of our room high in the trees meant we could see the line of fire flicker in panorama-vision as we lay on our bed. We watched for another anxious hour until the advance appeared to slow. We figured that the lodge management neither wanted to lose their property nor their guests to brushfire, so they'd give us plenty of warning if the situation became dangerous. Still, we laid out clothes and packed our passports, money, pills, and essentials into a small backpack that we could grab if we had to flee. Finally, we fell asleep, windows and doors open to the smell of distant smoke, hoping that someone would alert us in time to evacuate if that became necessary.

When we awoke the next morning, the fire was out, with just a slight haze of smoke visible and an acrid smell of ash on the breeze. We left camp soon after breakfast. The route to our next destination passed through the burned area. As we drove through acres of charred land, our guide revealed that camp staff and nearby villagers had spent most of the night clearing a long band of bush that stood in the path of the fire. The resulting narrow strip of bare dirt served as a firebreak that, stripped of fuel, stopped the fire in its tracks less than a mile from camp. Much too close for comfort.

Experience had taught us exactly what we were looking at when, a few years later, we caught sight of another glowing orange line in the distance one night. This time, we were staying in the Qorokwe concession in Botswana, far from any farming activity, leaving no doubt a lightning strike had ignited this fire. Although Botswana was experiencing a drought, the seasonal return of water into the Okavango Delta had begun, so the vegetation had absorbed some moisture.

Much smaller than the Tarangire blaze, this fire was also farther away from camp. While Mike and I were concerned, the situation didn't send our anxiety levels off the charts. Camp staff beat the fire out with blankets within hours. The following day, our guide, who had been part of the fire brigade, drove us by the stretch of blackened grassland where several patches of brush still smoldered.

The one positive about fires in the African plains and bush is that the grass returns quickly. As we've traveled in various national parks and wildlife concessions, we've seen herd animals feasting on green shoots pushing through the blackened debris of an earlier fire. In some places, we've even seen rangers do controlled burns to jump-start that cycle of new growth. We've seen similar controlled burns in India, South America, and the American West.

Through these brushes with danger, Mike and I have developed our own approach to travel. We stay on top of the news, domestic and international, to keep up to date on hot spots, whether man-made or natural, that might be flaring in the world. Before planning a trip, we review the US State Department warnings for a country or region, especially if we have some questions about safety there. We often continue to receive State Department alerts for countries we've visited in the past, and that helps us keep current if we contemplate returning at some point. Online travel boards where people comment about their trips and ask fellow travelers questions can also help provide firsthand information about a destination. We've used those forums to get traveler opinions about which of many beach towns to choose for a stay in Costa Rica or which house rental agencies are reputable.

Centers for Disease Control and Prevention (CDC) advisories for each country can also alert travelers in advance to diseases and other health and safety risks in particular regions. In Cambodia, I'd never have thought about avoiding chickens without having read the CDC guidance. But we traveled there shortly after China and Southeast Asia had destroyed thousands of chickens that were carriers for avian flu. It was handy to know that tidbit when we came across a flock of chickens occupying one of the many temples at Angkor Wat.

That phrase "knowledge is power" exists for a reason. When it comes to travel, knowledge comes from at least minimal research that can help give travelers the power to decide if they should visit a destination and what the risks are, if any. Of course, natural disasters, accidents, strikes/protests, and other disruptions happen everywhere. So, it's foolish to be surprised when such unexpected things happen during travel. We've been annoyed to encounter mishaps like these but not shocked. If my experiences can teach you anything, reader, research and be prepared for weather events and seismic activity if they are common in the country you're visiting. And know what to do if a dangerous natural event occurs. One more example: When we disembarked from our boat for a swim on a small island off the coast of Krabi, Thailand, we carefully read the big signs with directions to a path to higher ground in case of a tsunami.

Be Prepared. Knowledge is power.

"Afternoon Moon" by Mike Knowlton. Manda Island, Kenya. 2007

Close Encounters with Crime and Terrorism

W HEN TRAVELERS speak about the dangers of the road, crime and terrorism often emerge as key themes. Let's talk about crime first. The simple truth is, yes, there's crime in the United States, and there's crime abroad. And—if you're traveling to a place where the average yearly income is equal to the amount you spent at Starbucks last month—understand that, while most people are honest and good, for others, tourists present an irresistible temptation. Mostly for theft. Violent crime against tourists is much rarer, and Mike and I have never been threatened with bodily harm.

However, we have been victims of theft. On our first safari, one of our traveling companions had some items stolen from her open suitcase. Since then, we've made it a routine practice to lock our suitcases when we're out of our room, not just in Africa but everywhere, from a European River Cruise to Dallas to Laos. But we thought in-room safes were just that, safe—until we had cash stolen from our lockbox in a camp in southern Africa. Outstanding camp management and our travel company responded immediately and made sure we were made whole upon returning home. Still, it was a distressing experience that made us even more cautious about how we treat our valuables while traveling.

Josh eluded another version of attempted theft on a trip with a friend to Mexico's Riviera Maya. A local policeman stopped him for a supposed road violation and tried to shake him down with a fine, payable on the spot in cash. Josh and his travel companion insisted that they couldn't understand the cop's Spanish and kept saying they had a plane to catch.

Finally, out of frustration, the policeman let them go. On that same trip, Josh used our family American Express card for a few purchases. Imagine my shock when the next month's bill showed that he'd purchased $35,000 of Louis Vuitton luggage from a shop in Mexico City. In keeping with their excellent customer service, AmEx removed the charge from the card when we explained that Josh had been nowhere near Mexico City nor made a designer luggage purchase.

The most brazen theft we experienced happened one night in the lagoon of Bora Bora in French Polynesia's Society Islands. On the last stretch of a two-week sail through several islands, we spent the night anchored in a remote, peaceful spot away from Vaitape, the main town on Bora Bora. Mike and I slept like babies through the quiet night, hearing nothing but the wind, the frogs, and the waves lapping against the hull. Apparently, our captain slept just as soundly. What a surprise when we awoke to find that someone had paddled up to the sailboat during the night and made off with the dinghy.

Our captain reported the theft by radio to the authorities and our charter company but said that it would be fruitless to try to sail around and locate the stolen dinghy. Unfortunately, we had to make the long sail back to Raiatea without a dinghy, although we had an inflatable lifeboat on board for emergency use. Upon our return to port, we were relieved to hear that our boat insurance policy covered the cost of the stolen dinghy. Still, it couldn't cover the disquieting feeling that our idyllic Polynesian getaway had been violated by common theft. Or the lingering question: Would we have awakened if the stealthy thieves had climbed aboard to search for other loot or to cause harm? In certain areas of the world, piracy is a well-known concern. Sailors often avoid the southern reaches of the Caribbean. Commercial ship traffic is on alert near the coast of Somalia. However, we'd never thought about crime on the peaceful waters of Polynesia. The palm trees, hula girls, and smiling faces had lulled us into a false sense of security in Bora Bora's lagoon.

The threat of danger and necessity for caution have been much clearer in other specific places we've traveled. Back in the eighties, Mike took me along on a work-related conference to Acapulco, Mexico. I was excited to visit the famous beach destination, known for sultry nights, a fiesta vibe, and the young men who performed hair-raising dives from the cliffs into the sea. But since our days there had been tightly scheduled as part of the conference program, I did little advance research.

The reality was a shock. Yes, the beaches were lovely. But Acapulco was a sprawling city with many high-rise buildings. Somehow, I'd envisioned more of a sleepy little beach town like in the one in the Elizabeth Taylor–Richard Burton movie version of the Tennessee Williams play, *Night of the Iguana*. Or at least a frolic-in-the-sun vibe like the Elvis movie, *Fun in Acapulco*. Although the hotel décor did its best to invoke that Mexican holiday feel, at check-in, the conference staff immediately cautioned us against traveling on our own outside the hotel.

On our first day on the beach, I was appalled to see uniformed men patrolling the waterline with Uzis. I found it disturbing, and more than a little frightening, to lounge on a beach chair in my bathing suit and watch law enforcement shouldering these ugly black weapons of death stroll by on full alert. Acapulco was my first experience with men carrying assault weapons. I wish I could say it was my last.

One night, Mike and I boarded a conference bus to dine at a lovely restaurant on a hill overlooking the city. From that vantage point, the lights of Acapulco sparkled like gems and reflected in the dark sea beyond. But, as we drove back to the hotel, the streets were rife with homeless adults and children sleeping in doorways.

We did get to see the famous cliff divers, although even that was a bit of a circus. We had fun, but Acapulco became an early lesson in how some tourist destinations thrive on a carefully crafted illusion. Plus, the sight of Uzis on a sunny beach taught me that life could be more dangerous, even in lovely places, than in sedate Southcentral Pennsylvania.

Of course, times have changed. Now, the United States has become one of the gun hot spots of the world, with many countries cautioning their citizens about our gun culture in their travel advisories. But, at the time of our trip to Acapulco, America used rifles for hunting. Pistols were for cops and movie cowboys, and only gangsters and the military carried any armament that looked like a machine gun.

Since that long-ago Acapulco trip, we've visited other countries where guns are readily visible. In several African countries, we've been stopped at roadblocks by uniformed men with guns. And, although these road guardians almost always dress in camouflage, they're not always military or police. The people controlling the borders between countries work for governments. In other locations, it's often unclear if the men blocking the roads act with government authority or have seized control of that stretch of remote road simply because they can.

In Botswana, we saw the Botswana Defence Force's anti-poaching unit in action one day; at the time, this armed governmental military unit enforced a stringent anti-poaching policy, which the press referred to, somewhat overstated, as "shoot to kill." The resources they brought to the poaching incident the day we saw them were impressive. The soldiers' resolute faces as they barreled down the road would likely give any poacher pause.

Depending upon the individual country's rules, some of our African guides carried guns to protect against animal attacks; other countries did not permit guides to carry weapons. On a road trip into northcentral Kenya's Samburu National Park, our unarmed guides emphasized that we could only travel during daylight hours. Danger came at night from bandits who targeted vehicles on the road after dark. The potholes on that long road were so deep that a vehicle could disappear inside one—a perfect place for a bandit to stage a surprise attack. However, we made the trip in a long, straight drive (swerving only for those potholes) and arrived without mishap. It turned out that the biggest danger was the psychic assault from the very persistent hawkers who approached our vehicle every time we stopped in a small town, trying to persuade us to buy wooden carvings, beaded bracelets, and more. All right. I did buy a few trinkets. At almost every stop. But we arrived at our destination before dark and with no illegal bandit encounters.

Although we've rarely seen citizens in other countries carrying guns other than hunting rifles, we've visited countries with a very visible armed police or military presence. In Paris and some other European cities, military units patrolled tourist hot spots like Notre Dame or the Eiffel Tower. In Vietnam, we saw a lot of armed police officers and a substantial military contingent at some of the significant monuments in the north. Myanmar had similar uniformed and armed guards at residences of key officials and in the major cities. We've also had to navigate stringent security checks from armed law enforcement at places as diverse as the US Ambassador's home in Santiago, Chile, the US Embassy in Gaborone, Botswana, and the Grand Palace, home of the exquisite and priceless Emerald Buddha, in Bangkok, Thailand.

Fortunately, we've never had any run-ins with the law while traveling. Except for that incident of being pulled over by a policeman in New Zealand for driving too slowly I described earlier. Oh, and I shouldn't forget that one time with the Coast Guard.

Mike, Josh, and I were sailing from St. Croix to St. John in the US Virgin Islands, with an instructor, Captain Roger. If all went well, Roger would award each of us cruising certification, the last certification we needed to easily charter and sail a boat on our own. We were cruising along under sail in our fifty-foot yacht, minding our own business on a beautiful Caribbean afternoon. Then, a US Coast Guard patrol boat, 100+ feet with a serious-looking fixed gun in the prow, appeared on the horizon. Our first reaction was mild interest. We hadn't passed any other boats for a while. Seeing a Coast Guard cutter was a pleasant distraction in our long, open-water passage.

Then the patrol boat slowed, and the crew lowered a rigid-hull inflatable boat from the stern. As we continued to sail, we watched the activity with curiosity. After all, it was just the Coast Guard and us, alone in this open stretch of water midway between the two islands. Suddenly, our ship-to-ship radio crackled as the Coast Guard hailed us.

"Stand by for boarding," the Coast Guard captain announced. "Maintain your course and your speed. We will come alongside and board while you're underway."

Roger replied that we'd do as they said. What choice did we have?

As the inflatable, filled with a group of Coast Guardsmen, sped toward us, they motored in a wide arc so they could come up alongside our boat. We held course and speculated about what was happening. Were they bored and just using us for practice? Or, as Roger suggested, did we look like drug runners, and they were boarding to look for contraband? We were sailing in waters well known for drug smuggling.

None of us had drugs on board, but the idea of being searched, no matter how innocent I might be, had my heart pounding.

The inflatable continued to gain on us. When just a few moments away from boarding our boat, the inflatable stopped and drifted back. The Coastie on the helm turned to peer at the outboards.

As we watched some frantic activity from the crew involving the inflatable engines, the radio crackled for a second time. "Proceed," the Coast Guard vessel radioman told Roger. "We will not be boarding your boat."

All that drama and suspense, only to have it end abruptly because of a mechanical breakdown! I've always wondered how many real drug runners escape because of Coast Guard engine malfunction.

Terrorism is an unfortunate fact of life for travelers in this era. Mike and I have taken the position that we won't be foolhardy about traveling into terrorist hot spots, but we want to travel and accept that the journey comes with certain risks. So, no, we wouldn't plan a pleasure jaunt into Yemen or Syria during their wars, but, yes, we will go to France or London or New York even though they've been the focus of multiple terrorist attacks.

Sometimes, that means we've had near misses. Our last visit to France included several days in Paris. We visited Notre Dame[5] one afternoon and commented to each other about the strong presence of anti-terrorist patrols. Small groups of heavily armed police (or military) passed us several times during our time in the Île de la Cité. Two weeks later, we'd just returned home from Provence when we saw news reports of those patrols thwarting a terrorist bombing on the cathedral. Those arrested were ISIS sympathizers.

Similarly, we knew that unrest and terrorism had been a fact of life in East Africa for many years. The northernmost country in the region, Somalia, hasn't been a viable tourist destination for decades. For over a quarter of a century, starvation, strife, and violence have reigned throughout the nation. In the early 1990s, America helped provide food

---

5 Prior to the fire that devastated the cathedral in April 2019.

relief to more than a quarter-million starving Somalis. However, most people only remember America's involvement in that attempt to help the war-torn country as the battle of Mogadishu chronicled in Mark Bowden's novel *Black Hawk Down* or the subsequent movie.

Al Shabab, an East African Al Qaeda offshoot, emerged from the ashes of Somalia's continuing instability in early 2006 to become a sporadic presence in Kenya, Tanzania, Uganda, Mozambique, and Somalia. The jihadist group's most notable attacks included the 2013 siege on Nairobi's high-end West Gate shopping mall, killing sixty-seven. Their deadliest attack, a truck bombing in Mogadishu, killed almost 600 people in 2017. In 2019, the group targeted a luxury tourist hotel in, again, Nairobi, killing twenty-one. However, for various reasons, the more remote safari destinations have not been targeted by Al Shabab.

We took our first safari to Kenya in 2009, well before Al Shabaab made its first major incursions into the country. At the end of our safari, we spent five days on beautiful Manda Island off the mainland. This Indian Ocean beach resort is located near the more famous jet-set destination of Lamu Island but was quiet and glorious. The perfect end to more than two weeks on safari. We stayed in a soaring thatched-roof "hut" on the beach, visited the ancient Islamic city of Lamu on market day, and enjoyed a romantic dinner under the stars at a table on the beach at low tide. We kicked back with sundowners on the top of a hill with a 360-degree view of the ocean and the bay, set up with couches and an expert to identify the southern latitude's stars as they emerged. Mike and I marked the resort as "will return" because we had a wonderful stay, even though we could see the not-too-distant coast of Somalia from our veranda.

But that desire to return came crashing down when we received an email from the resort two years later. They had decided to close temporarily for safety reasons after militants killed a French tourist living in his second home on the far side of Manda Island. The militants, believed to be Al Shabaab, kidnapped his disabled wife and took her to Somalia, where she later died. This tragedy happened just two weeks after a British couple was kidnapped farther north on the Kenyan coast. So, our beloved resort shut down.

This lodging has since reopened, but the peace was marred yet again in 2020 when Al Shabaab attacked a US/Kenyan joint military base on Manda Island. We would love to return to this beach paradise someday but will wait and hope the danger from Somali militants and pirates subsides.

Our second safari in Kenya was in late 2017, four years after the West Gate Mall attack and two years after a more targeted Al Shabab attack on a school in northeastern Kenya. We believed the country safe, especially where we planned to spend most of our time in the remote Masai Mara and beyond. However, to be cautious, we chose to spend our two nights in the Nairobi area in a lodge in Karen, a residential area on the outskirts of the city. Once more rural, the suburb is named for Karen Blixen, who wrote about her days on a Kenyan coffee farm in the book *Out of Africa*. I loved staying there since the tale of Blixen, her faithless baron husband, her lover Denys Finch-Hatton, and her later rival for Denys's affections, Beryl Markham, is a true-life romance that has long fascinated me. Paula McClain has also written an excellent book about Markham called *Circling the Sun*, which tells the story from the younger woman's perspective.

I watched the movie *Out of Africa* starring Meryl Streep and Robert Redford so often in the nineties that my teenage son would roll his eyes and tease me by quoting the opening line in a mock Blixen/Streep Danish accent, "I had a farm in Africa . . ." As it turns out, the grown-up Josh enjoyed staying in Karen for a few days before we headed out on safari.

When it comes to the threat of terrorism, I believe travelers can strike a balance. Practically no place on earth seems to be free of that threat. For years, we here in America liked to talk about Islamic terrorism as if it's the only thing we had to fear. Without a doubt, it is a real threat, as 9/11 demonstrated so tragically. Sporadic military base shootings and lone-wolf attacks by Islamic fundamentalist sympathizers continue to underscore that the threat of international terrorism persists here at home. Major ISIS-affiliated attacks in Paris, London, Nice, and elsewhere show that terrorists remain active across the globe.

But Americans' chance of being killed by home-grown white supremacist terrorists has become the biggest danger on US soil.[6] Our government officials and reports from the FBI and Homeland Security warn about the rising threat of domestic terrorism. The 2021 attack on the US Capitol and the litany of recent mass shootings and anti-government violence have only made this threat more visible.

In my mind, the balance I believe we should try to maintain, whether dealing with international or domestic terrorism, has three central tenets. These work well to minimize the likelihood of falling victim to crime as well.

First, **DON'T BE COMPLETELY CLUELESS**, i.e., hiking in the mountains of Iran, no matter how beautiful, is just not a wise move right now. Or if there's an active terrorist alert in a major city, consider forgoing that soccer playoff.

Second, **STAY ALERT**. When touring a museum or grand cathedral, it's easy to develop 'tourist brain' and become so enraptured by art, history, or religious devotion that we forget to pay attention to our surroundings and fellow tourists. One of the best pieces of advice I've embraced comes from Mitch Rapp, the swashbuckling spy and superhero from Vince Flynn's action-adventure series. Rapp emphasized how important it is for fliers to read the emergency card in the seatback, pay attention to the safety briefing, and study the layout of the plane/emergency exits. I've always taken that example in its broader context. Don't be a passive traveler. Be prepared and be aware of what's happening around you.

Third, **DON'T BECOME SO OVERWHELMED BY FEAR AND THE POSSI-BILITIES OF "WHAT IF"** that you let travel pass you by. It's more likely that some threat of terrorism or violence will still exist in the world when you're eighty-five than it is that you'll still have the stamina and enthusiasm for travel to exotic places at that age.

Carpe diem, and the terrorists be damned.

---

6 Eileen Sullivan and Katie Benner, "Top law enforcement officials say the biggest domestic terror threat comes from white supremacists." *New York Times,* June 15, 2021. https://www.nytimes.com/2021/05/12/us/politics/domestic-terror-white-supremacists.html.

"Polar Bears at Play" by Mike Knowlton. Hudson Bay near Churchill, Manitoba, Canada. 2013

Close Encounters of the Animal Kind

IKE AND I love to go on trips where we'll see wildlife. As I
mentioned in the chapter on hiking, bears are one of the biggest animal dangers on the trail. But, when we expanded our
horizons to other wild places in the world, like parts of Africa, India,
Indonesia, and even Canada, we had to be on our guard for a whole new
universe of threatening animals.

To continue with an earlier bear theme, one of our most shocking
introductions to a destination occurred in Manitoba, Canada. We had
come to Churchill to view polar bears during their annual migration
from the interior onto Hudson Bay as the ice freezes. When our group
arrived at the airport in midmorning, a local greeter drew our tour guides
aside for a whispered conversation. A few minutes later, our group leaders, their faces ashen, returned to brief us.

Earlier that morning, in the village, a mother polar bear, her cub, and
a male who could have been her juvenile offspring had attacked three
people leaving a Halloween party in the wee hours. The mother bear attacked one of the women and began dragging her away. A male neighbor,
hearing the commotion and screams, rushed outside, picked up a shovel,
and started to beat the bear in an attempt to end the attack. Distracted,
the bear dropped the woman and pounced on her rescuer. Then two ad-
ditional men arrived on the scene; one fired a gun with "crackers" aimed
to frighten the bear away. The other jumped in his pick-up and drove
toward the bear, eventually scaring it off.

Conservation officers tracked the fleeing mama bear, killing both her and the juvenile male. The officers followed the province policy of putting down all polar bears that attack humans. The officers sedated the cub with a dart gun and took him to Winnipeg's zoo to live his life in captivity. The two severely injured villagers were airlifted to Winnipeg for treatment. Both lived, but the woman had the back of her scalp and part of an ear mauled off, three arteries severed, and needed numerous stitches. Her rescuer lost an ear and suffered severe lacerations on his legs and back. He later received a heroism award and recalled being grateful that he'd landed on his stomach during the mauling, thinking, "Where is that son-of-a-bitch going to bite me next?' He's starting to eat."[7]

Some of these details we pieced together during our week in Churchill since the attack dominated conversation everywhere in the small village. Some we learned back in Winnipeg in a conversation with a National Geographic film crew that also had been in the area right after the attack. The rest we read in the news upon our return home.

Sometimes, the polar bears, like those in this deadly incident, arrive before Hudson Bay is completely frozen, so they just hang around the area waiting for the ice to form. This attack was somewhat unusual because Churchill is fully on alert for polar bear intrusions. Manitoba employs a full-time crew of conservation officers to keep these dangerous animals out of town during the peak migration months. If bears come into populated areas, the rangers scare them away with noisemakers. If any bears become repeat offenders, the rangers dart them with sedatives and put them in Bear Jail, a Quonset hut-like structure with strong holding pens for unruly bruins. Sometimes, after a few days' stay, the bears are released. But occasionally, bears released from jail return to town. We watched rangers load one such bear into a net and airlift it by helicopter to a more remote location. All polar bears in jail are set free when the ice is fully frozen. For these hungry bruins who've eaten little over the summer months, the lure of tasty seals out on the frozen bay clears them out of town as soon as the ice is thick enough to navigate.

---

7 Paul Hunter, "He saved a woman from a polar bear. 'Then the mauling was on for me'" *Toronto Star*, May 20, 2017. https://www.thestar.com/news/insight/2017/05/20/he-saved-a-woman-from-a-polar-bear-then-the-mauling-was-on-for-me.html.

However, the family involved in the attack had slipped through the cracks, strolling into the village just twenty minutes after the last patrol had completed their rounds. The mother bear likely acted to protect her cub when surprised by the three early morning revelers.

After hearing the news about the potential danger, we paid close attention when told that the citizens of snowy Churchill always leave the doors of both their homes and cars unlocked. While out walking, we understood we were to step into the nearest house or jump into a parked vehicle if a bear approached.

We were very wary when walking around town but experienced only one scare on the outskirts by the water. Our group had to make an emergency return to our minibus when a bear took a turn toward us as rangers tried to chase it out of the village. All of us scurried back to the bus, constantly glancing over our shoulders as the bear sprinted in our direction, fleeing the firecracker pops of the rangers' noisemakers. We all managed to get into the vehicle before the bear reached us. From our safe haven, we watched as the rangers' jeep appeared and herded the bear away from town.

Another place that had me jumpy when we stepped ashore was Rinca Island in the Indonesian archipelago. On a sailing cruise, we stopped there to see the famed Komodo dragons, giant lethal lizards that live only on four neighboring islands, including Komodo, from which they derive their name. These babies are ginormous, many of them reaching eight feet long and a hundred fifty pounds in weight. The bacteria in their mouths have long been believed to be the most dangerous feature of the dragons. Since our trip, that theory has largely been discounted, and scientific debate now focuses on whether venom or a combination of the bites, blood loss, and environmental factors hasten the death of their prey. Regardless, the dragons' bites are lethal. The giant lizards attack their prey, such as water buffalo, and then simply step back and wait for the wounds to kill their victims before they move in for the feast.

While sailing to Rinca, our guides provided a safety briefing to prepare us for hiking on the island. They instructed us to stay well away from the big dragons, many of which we'd see in one area near the ranger station. Although the creatures look slow and sluggish, they can quickly rush their prey—including random tourists. However, we were told not to worry; the island rangers hiked with poles to deter the dragons if they approached.

Then came the unexpected news. Our guides advised us to be especially careful if we walked under trees. Smaller, one-to-three-foot-long juvenile dragons like to hang out in the limbs and sometimes jump onto hikers' backs. "Although the dragon kids are smaller than the full-grown adults, their saliva is just as dangerous," they said. Eek! Suddenly, the expression "leaping lizards" didn't seem so cute.

Several rangers met us at the docks and gave us instructions that echoed what we'd been told the day before. They were all big guys in uniform who sounded like they knew what they were doing. Somewhat worrying, however, was that their "protective equipment" turned out to be slender tree branches, maybe an inch in diameter and eight feet long with a small Y at the ground end of the stick. All that stood between us and a giant lizard with lethal saliva was little more than a hiking pole!

We saw a lot of Komodos just a few minutes inland at the ranger station complex. These adults were very large. Most of them were just resting, but a few jockeyed with each other for prime basking spots. And when they moved, it was fast.

After that introduction to the Komodo dragons, Mike and I split up. He went on the longer hike into the island's hills and saw quite a few larger dragons on the walk. I opted for the more leisurely stroll, which took us through—wait for it—a grove of trees. I spent the entire time scanning the branches overhead for small Komodos. It's a miracle I didn't trip and break a leg since my gaze was directed upward at the tree limbs for most of the walk. We did spot a few of the little guys. I wish I could say they were totally adorbs, but that whole lethal-if-they-bite-you-aspect tempered the cute factor.

Seeing these legendary creatures in the wild was quite fascinating. And it turns out that the rangers' sticks did seem to deter advances by even the biggest of the Komodos. Still, I breathed a sigh of relief as we stood on the dock waiting for our dinghy back to the boat. That's when I remembered the dragons can swim . . .

In some of the wild places we've visited, walking on our own invited danger and sometimes even violated the rules. For example, in India, most national parks didn't allow us to step outside the vehicle, except at designated rest stops. Tigers can be savage and aren't to be trifled with. We stayed at a lodge in Tadoba National Park near where the big cats had killed three villagers in recent months, all farmers sleeping in their fields. But tigers weren't the only peril. At night, the young boys who staffed the camps walked around the lodge tapping sticks on the sidewalks to scare away wandering gaur, a type of bison, and leopards on the prowl. We learned that the warnings were justified when we watched a colossal gaur pass through the lodge grounds at dusk one evening.

In the African bush, even around the camps, we soon learned to stay on the lookout for random animals passing through. We've had everything from elephants and hippos to leopards, kudu, and Cape buffalo wander by our tents both day and night. The general rules are don't step outside at night, and in daylight wait inside until they move on or—if that's not possible—take a big detour if you encounter one of these beasts.

We have gone on walking safaris (the term for hikes in the African bush), always with a guide or knowledgeable local, sometimes with a rifle for protection. Rangers, tourists, and locals are killed every year by wildlife in countries like Tanzania and Botswana, which have concentrations of wild animals. Every guide we've met has emphasized the need to be cautious in the bush, but a lunch stop in Uganda brought that home in real-time. One day, our group of ten had stopped for lunch under a tree while on a game drive. As we were finishing our meal, one of the guides looked around the group and asked, "Where's Drake?" In an offhand voice, his wife said, "Oh, he went down to the river to do some tai-chi."

I'll never forget the looks of shock and alarm on both of the guides' faces. We all scanned the riverbank, about a half-mile away, where we could see a tall figure doing poses by the water's edge. The guides yelled a few panicked words about crocodiles and hippos as they leaped into one of the safari vehicles. Commanding the rest of us to stay put and remain alert, they sped toward the river to collect our fellow traveler and bundle him into the Land Rover. He was fine, but the incident prompted a detailed lecture about the dangers of wandering away from the vehicle or camps.

I'd harbored no real inclination to defy the rules. But, if I had, the guides' horrified expressions would have been enough to convince me of the danger. Just before they rode to the rescue, the glance they exchanged with each other managed to convey several thoughts: *OMG, these stupid tourists; I fear for our charge's safety; if Drake gets attacked by a croc, hippo, or lion, we'll lose our guide licenses and our livelihoods.*

Our most frightening experience in Africa came on the beautiful, tranquil waters of Botswana's Okavango Delta. Mike and I were cruising by motorboat, captained by our guide, Josef, down a narrow channel when a rogue hippo rushed our boat. He swam straight at us, stopping just a few feet away to open his mouth in a tremendous roar.[8]

When the animal rushed us again and again, Josef raced the boat to the shallows next to a small island, trying to make it harder for the hippo to get under the boat to flip it then attack us in the water. He told my husband and me to get ready to dash to a nearby palm tree and climb it. The gravity of our situation hit with lightning speed when I weighed the odds of my reaching that tree, chased by an enraged animal with the size and speed of a small car. Slim to none.

Still, the hippopotamus charged closer and closer. On the beast's last run, he leaped, head and shoulders out of the water, dampening us with spray. His mouth yawned so wide we saw every inch of his two-foot incisors. Just as we prepared to ditch the boat and run for that tree, the hippo backed off. The guide jammed the boat into gear and fled with the hippo in pursuit. As we rounded a bend in the channel, the hippo abandoned the chase at long last.

That hippo encounter may well have been the most terrifying experience in my life. Not only was I petrified, but the situation also made me acutely aware of my physical limitations. If we'd been forced to leave the boat and run for that scrawny palm tree, there was a good chance the hippo would have flattened me. Being trampled and chomped by an angry hippo didn't sound like a particularly attractive way to die.

I didn't scream, faint, cry, or blubber. Instead, I channeled much of my fear into worry for my husband, who continued to shoot photos each time the hippo leaped at us. I held it together under pressure.

---

[8] A note: Rogue hippos are solitary males cast out of the pod (family group). Living alone makes them ill-tempered and very dangerous. Hippos kill more people in Africa each year than any other large animal. (https://lowvelder.co.za/245166/10-dangerous-animals-africa).

Afterward, a shaken Josef confided, "This was one of the closest calls I'd had with a rogue hippo." His original plan had been to retrace our steps and use the same waterway on the return to camp. Instead, he rerouted to a series of narrow channels that circumvented the hippo. Because the Delta water level was falling at that time of year, some of those channels were so shallow that he jumped out of the boat and pulled it with a rope—like Humphrey Bogart towing the African Queen but with a smaller craft.

I've been wary of hippos both in the water and on land ever since that Okavango experience. But I view the hippo encounter and the other brushes with dangerous wild animals as a valuable series of lessons. When in the wild, I have entered the animals' world, so I need to respect them and proceed with caution. Usually, wild animals prefer not to confront humans, but most will attack if cornered. Ignoring that reality can be fatal. We've all read articles or seen videos of that tourist trying to take a picture with a bison and getting gored or that mama grizzly mauling a hiker who got between her and her cubs. They act from instinct because they are—as the tourists discover the hard way—wild animals.

I find that stepping into an animal-dominated environment can provide a perspective that's both refreshing and sobering. Humans like to think that we're the dominant creatures on earth. However, confronting a tiger or polar bear in the wild, one-on-one, can quickly challenge the limits of that theory.

"Eyes of a Child" by Mike Knowlton. Village on the Amazon, Upper Amazon Basin, Peru. 2008

13

People to People

ONE OF the best things about traveling is meeting people from different countries and cultures and learning more about how they live. Several times, we've rented houses for a week or two in Italy and France. More recently, we've spent more than a month on two different Caribbean islands. Living in a community, even for a short time, has given us a chance to meet locals, find the rhythm of a foreign place, and develop more insight into a culture.

Too often in our travels the interaction with local people is more fleeting, but sometimes even the briefest interaction can be memorable. And our guides, who almost always hail from the nations we're visiting, have taught us a lot about their countries and ways of life. On longer trips, we found that a level of familiarity and trust often builds during the excursion, and the guide will become franker in describing a country's government or economy over time.

Small group tours often allow interaction with residents through scheduled time in area villages, schools, or even homes. These visits sometimes have a staged element and almost always benefit the locals financially, whether through payment for their time, a sales opportunity, or a donation of school supplies. Other times, these visits often allow for genuine interaction, even with language barriers and limited translators.

Mike and I have had the chance to speak with local people in many countries, sometimes with the help of an interpreter. Our small-village visits include spots as varied as remote Indonesian islands; the banks of the Amazon; Masai and Samburu villages in Tanzania and Kenya;

floating villages in northern Vietnam and Cambodia; Andean villages in the Sacred Valley of Peru; and farming villages in India. We've also explored blazing white horas in Greece and more Tuscan and Umbrian hill towns and Provençal hamlets than I can count. We've wandered through big cities and towns, where we've chatted with shopkeepers, hoteliers, market vendors, and more. Visiting ramshackle slums in Soweto, near Johannesburg, South Africa, gave us a chance to talk to three young men who'd lived their whole lives in huts without running water or plumbing. They cautioned us not to touch the live wire hanging from the ceiling, which supplied their electricity, pirated from a transmission line nearby.

I've really enjoyed the school visits in Laos, Uganda, Tanzania, Indonesia, and Peru, where smiling children get a kick out of reciting their ABCs or singing a song for their visitors, usually in their native languages. The exception was on Bali, an island where almost everyone we met was kind and welcoming. But the preteen boys at the school where we stopped had mastered using the middle finger to register their displeasure at being displayed as a tourist attraction. I could see their point. I suppose their response also proves that flippant twelve-year-old boys like to push the limits even in the most serene of cultures.

Through all these opportunities to meet people where they live and work, we've developed a better appreciation for the fact that most of the world does not live the way we do in America. (Of course, the way we live in the United States varies depending upon region, income level, and more.) We've traveled through much of Montana on visits to my brother. In some stretches, we'd pass a house and drive an hour before we passed another. Very different than even the most rural areas of our home state of Pennsylvania. Worlds away from Miami or New York City. And those places all differ from the small, remote villages in Alaska that one can only reach by floatplane.

Even the most poverty-stricken neighborhoods in the United States—and I've seen many up close during the government phase of my career—have better infrastructure and living standards than many situations in developing nations. Seeing kids beg on the streets of Mumbai, passing acres of tin-roofed shanties without indoor plumbing on the outskirts of Nairobi, or walking through homes and villages both urban and rural from Peru to Southeast Asia to Indonesia can be eye-opening.

Witnessing such poverty broadened my perspective on the world. Reading the daily news takes on a much more personal element when I've walked in the place featured in the story and talked to people who could be impacted by a natural disaster or outbreak of violence there.

Sometimes, the best people experiences are the ones we stumble across. On our first trip to Mumbai, we were on a walking tour of one area of the city. Our guide stopped at a Jain temple to show us the difference between this religious sect's temples and the many Hindu and Buddhist temples we'd visited earlier. He was surprised to find a wedding in progress and told us we were out of luck and would be unable to enter. However, one of the family members came out, spoke to the guide, and invited our small group into the ceremony. There, we watched the lavishly dressed bride and groom as they sat together on a small dais, listened to some readings by a priest, and joined in lighting candles and presenting the bride with small gifts. I found the entire scene dazzling; women and men alike wore brightly colored clothing adorned with beads. The young couple on the dais were surrounded by friends and family. Candles flickered. Flowers, mostly the ever-present marigolds of India, filled the room. And the table in the center of the room sagged under the pile of gifts that would be presented to the bride and groom during the ceremony.

After less than an hour, we left. The wedding ceremony would continue for another several days. But I'll never forget that couple and their families. How gracious to invite a group of strangers as guests into their important celebration, even if for just a while.

In Kathmandu, we went to Durbar Square to visit the Living Goddess. In this Nepali tradition, embraced by Buddhists and Hindus, a young girl, usually six years old, is selected using a set of timeworn criteria to become the Kumari Devi, the Living Goddess. Families are, apparently, quite willing to give up their daughter to this great honor, and she goes to live with priests in a dedicated house in Kathmandu. One of her primary duties involves bestowing blessings upon the faithful. Even the President and Prime Minister of Nepal come to obtain her blessing each year. When the Living Goddess reaches puberty, she returns to her parents and goes back to living an ordinary life, while a new Living Goddess assumes her duties in Kathmandu. When we received the Living God-dess's blessing, we walked into a center room in the house, which was open to the third floor. The goddess appeared on the top floor balcony and made some hand gestures. Then, we gave our donation and left. Just seeing the deity is considered to bring good fortune.

When we continued to Durbar Square, we ran into a large group of young girls and their mothers. The girls were clad in elaborate red dresses. Kohl rimmed their eyes, and their small frames dripped with gold jewelry. These young Newaris were all gussied up for their Bel Bibaha marriage—a ceremony that marries them to a bel fruit, a symbol for the Hindu god Vishnu. As they age, girls are married a second time to the Sun and, finally, to a man in the more traditional sense. While we didn't fully understand all the nuances of this traditional ceremony, the pageantry and the young girls' excitement were fun to watch. And the mothers fussing over their daughters to make sure their dresses and make-up were just perfect felt very familiar.

Another incredible opportunity to interact with locals came in a small Ugandan village on a visit to the local witch doctor. We spent an hour and a half with this wizened old man in a battered green trench coat as he introduced us to the plants and other items he uses for his medical treatments and spells. We never discovered if the World War II-era green trench coat was a symbol of the witch doctor's status in the village or simply an unusual fashion choice given the warm weather. However, even with his remarks translated into English by our guide, the old man's self-assurance, humor, and sense of position came through. His techniques involved dispensing powders to sprinkle around a house to keep away evil spirits or love potions to encourage romance. Villagers do, however, rely on many of his traditional medicines while also seeking out more westernized medical treatments for more severe illnesses.

The witch doctor took quite a fancy to one of the single women in our group. She showed good humor at first, treating his attention as casual flirtation. But things took a more serious turn when he raised the prospect of children. He lost interest when she told him she wasn't seeking to become a mother. Fooled by her salon-dyed red hair, he hadn't realized that this sixty-something woman was well past her child-bearing years. Alas, the budding romance ended as quickly as it had begun.

When we left the witch doctor's hilltop hut to return to our vehicle, we discovered a huge event taking place in an open area near the parking lot. All the local school children were gathered for an award ceremony. Presiding district school officials lined up at a table in the front insisted that the American travelers be their guests at the ceremony. They brought us chairs and placed us near the officials' table to watch the awards presentation and several musical performances by the children. Near the end, the kids danced to drum music and pulled me up to join them. Great memory.

On another trip, this one to Tanzania, two of the tribes we visited invited my son to dance with them. Maasai warriors are known for their ability to launch themselves several feet in the air from a standing position. Josh, who was working as a professional modern dancer in New York City at the time, had a hard time matching the warriors' height above the ground when they challenged him to a jumping competition. Still, he did better than any of the other men in our group. Later in the same trip, Hadzabe bushmen invited Josh and others to an archery competition, followed by a dance. No leaping was involved in either event.

Mike and I witnessed another bushman tribe, the San of the Kalahari, perform a fascinating tribal dance one night at Jack's Camp in Botswana. We sat around a campfire in the wild and watched the bushmen trance dance. They circled the fire, slapping their bare feet against the sand in a hypnotic ritual that is a bushman tradition. Under the influence of the spirits and possibly something more potent, the tribe danced as if transported. Several times, one of the dancers would convulse and fall to the ground. Sitting in pitch dark with only the flickering fire illuminating the rhythmic pounding of feet on the desert sand was such an elemental experience. Although I was only an observer, the flames, the dancers, the rhythm, and the dark African wild held me spellbound in the mesmerizing mystery of the trance dance.

We've eaten a few dinners at locals' homes as part of small group tours. Often, the language barrier made these meals awkward. We went

"Hadzabe Bushman" by Mike Knowlton. Near Lake Eyasi, Tanzania. 2010

"Bel Bibaha Bride" by Mike Knowlton. Kathmandu, Nepal. 2011

"Balinese Grandmother" by Mike Knowlton. Bali, Indonesia. 2012

"Peruvian School Boys" by Mike Knowlton. Sacred Valley, Peru. 2008

to a home on an Indonesian island that turned out to be less a dinner with the family than a brief interaction with the translator, and then the family served us the meal. That experience felt more like a business transaction masquerading as a family dinner. A similar meal in a Ugandan guest house included a young girl from the family who spoke English. She dined with us while the rest of the family kept us supplied with a stream of native dishes. Both were interesting experiences but fell well short of a "dinner with a local family" as billed. However, we had lunch in a stilt house on Inle Lake in Myanmar, which was quite relaxed and interesting. Our hostess spoke English and shared fascinating details of life in a home raised over the water of this remote lake. And in Ireland, a married couple cooked us shepherd's pie and entertained us with anecdotes about life in Killarney.

Another time in the Sacred Valley of Peru, our group tour visited a Quechua woman's home to learn how the locals made their wildly popular drink, *chicha*, a corn-based beer. We missed some of the most unsavory parts of the brewing process, which often involves mastication of the main ingredients, but an oversize kettle of the finished product sat in the corner of her kitchen. She gave each of us a small cup of chicha to sample. Perhaps this fermented brew is an acquired taste, but based on the number it did on my digestive tract, my fervent advice is: Don't drink the chicha!

On a barge cruise of Burgundy, the captain and his wife took Mike, me, and our fellow travelers to her parents' house for dinner one night. What a lovely evening. After a tour of their home just outside a small village, we gathered in their dining room for a series of tasty courses and great conversation. Mom and Dad spoke no English. While Betty and I trotted out our rusty high school/college French, Mike and Steve didn't know a word of the language. But between the captain and his wife translating, Betty and I doing our best to remember the right words, and all of us employing hand gestures, we communicated just fine. That meal truly felt like dinner with a local family.

Mike and I enjoyed another memorable dinner when sailing in Polynesia. Our sailboat captain took us to a *motu* (small island) on the edge of the Taha'a Lagoon. The husband and wife who lived there cooked a meal over the fire, a fish he'd caught earlier in the day, along with other local dishes. We ate in a small, open-air pavilion with our captain translating our English and the combination of French and pidgin spoken by the couple. After watching a spectacular sunset, we took the dinghy back to our sailboat. I loved the rustic meal even though I'm not all that keen on fish!

Although I have Pollyanna tendencies, I must note that not everything I've learned about other cultures is positive. Sometimes walking a city street or at a popular tourist site overseas can feel more like running the gauntlet than enjoying the new experience. Street vendors, beggars, people offering to guide me or sell me drugs, scam artists, and pickpockets have all dimmed the luster of a simple stroll or my first glimpse of a stunning World Heritage Site. Even understanding that I'm in a poverty-stricken country and knowing that selling trinkets to tourists puts food on their table can't always offset the discomfiting experience of having persistent street vendors follow me around. After all, I can't buy from every vendor I encounter, and many times they're selling something I just don't need or want. Sometimes, not engaging at all works, but to me, that always seems so rude. A firm "No" can often, but not always, end it. I've learned that, in most situations, a halfhearted no or, even worse, admiring the vendor's product is the wrong thing to do—unless you genuinely want to buy. I've been known to buy a trinket from a particularly persistent or forlorn salesperson just to end the interaction. My friend Betty and I once had an artist follow us from temple to temple in Myanmar. We'd say, "No, thank you," to his proffered art and move onto another temple. But, surprise, when we emerged from that temple, he'd approach us again with a hopeful expression and new sales pitch. By the fourth temple, he'd worn us down. The hand-painted picture of monks robed in saffron is now hanging in our sunroom, where I see it every day and think of that persistent young man framed by the ancient temples of Bagan. On a recent visit to Betty's home, I smiled to see the similar painting she bought that day filling a prominent spot on her breakfast room wall.

In the early days of our travel, I naively expected that the people in remote villages would be unsophisticated craftsmen who sold their wares

"Street Musician" by Mike Knowlton. Raj Mahal Palace, Orchha, India. 2011

as a sideline. I now realize that poverty can make rabid capitalists of everyone from Maasai tribespeople to Ribereños in the remotest regions of the Amazon. I almost always buy something when we stop at a village where the locals make handicrafts. And, where bartering is expected, I usually let the villagers get the better of me; a couple of dollars more on a trip costing thousands is negligible to me but could make a huge difference to the villager.

But we've also been in situations where buying from one vendor creates hard feelings among the competition. I remember a Maasai village where I bought a few carvings from one vendor and some beaded work from another. Soon, I had several other women tugging my wrist toward their blankets full of carvings and beads. Yet, I couldn't possibly buy from all of them and fit the purchases into my small suitcase. Even more contentious, in a remote Lao village, I bought two handwoven table runners from one woman. Another woman got furious when I declined to buy anything from her and started to scream at me in Lao. The guide had to intervene.

Another cultural practice that can be quite disturbing involves the attitude of men toward women. Although we've traveled in several places much more patriarchal than the United States, the only country where I've found the gender attitudes truly uncomfortable has been India. Most of the other countries simply remind me of life during my fifties childhood when men dominated and women had fewer rights. Even in the few majority Muslim countries we've visited, while I may not endorse the role that women occupy, the rules are clear, dictate women's clothing, and impose constraints on men's interactions with females. Out of respect for the culture, I can deal with a few weeks of fifties *deja vu* or clear religious or societal rules, even though they may not be practices I endorse.

But I find India more disconcerting, especially in midsize and rural towns. Groups of men have followed me around, invaded my space, and asked personal questions. I understand that the American definition of an acceptable question for strangers can differ from an Indian one. But, several times, I've felt very uncomfortable in these situations. I particularly remember a stop in a midsize town in Madhya Pradesh during market day. Our group wandered through the market, and for a while, another woman and I separated from our husbands as we browsed. We were two middle-aged women, but still, a group of Indian men surrounded us and kept pressing closer and closer as they asked questions.

"Are you married?"

"How old are you?"

"How much money do you make?"

"Where's your husband?"

Finally, Mike came to our rescue. When he appeared on the scene, the men backed off. I don't believe we were in physical danger, but it was not a good feeling. In this and other encounters, especially in groups of men, there can be a very sexist and sexual vibe. It's clear that the Western concepts of personal space, sexual harassment, and respect for women are not commonplace. I would note that my one-on-one interactions with Indian men have been much less problematic.

Not unexpectedly, traveling can bring uncomfortable situations. Unfamiliar customs; a language I don't understand; signs I can't read; money my mind just can't convert to US dollars fast enough when making a purchase or bargaining with a vendor; foods that are too spicy or look like nothing I've ever eaten. On top of all that, I'm often exhausted after traveling across multiple time zones. All these factors can make a travel situation feel a little like stepping into the Twilight Zone. That feeling can be even more disorienting in a world where I can start my morning at home and go to bed in a foreign country. For me, most of these crazy and exotic experiences, even when they're a bit uncomfortable, draw me to travel. How dull would life be without challenges?

14

Travelers Well Met

I n *Tom Sawyer Abroad* by Mark Twain, Tom says, "I have found out there ain't no surer way to find out whether you like people or hate them than to travel with them." Truer words have never been written. I've traveled with long-time friends, and it's worked out beautifully. We've had a great time together. In a few instances, a trip has revealed that our traveling companions will stay better friends if we confine our friendship to home. However, Mike and I have discovered over the years that some of our closest friends are interested in traveling only to more "on the beaten path" destinations and others have no interest in traveling at all. A few friends and family have flat out told us that we're "crazy" to travel to some of the places we go. On the other hand, we've cobbled together a few trips with friends and family that turn out to be just wonderful. And our son and daughter-in-law are usually up for any journey we propose.

Lucky for us, we've met many people on the road who are as excited about travel as we are. We've also found that most hardcore travelers are outgoing when they meet in locations around the world. So, we've often had delightful conversations at dinner with strangers or formed an instant bond with another couple who's sharing our safari vehicle or sitting across the aisle on a train tour. On our first trip around the country during an extended stay in Jackson Hole, Wyoming, we struck up a friendship with two young Mormon men doing their two-year missions. An odd mix, perhaps, these two earnest young men and two long-haired hippies. But Mike worked with them at a local bakery, and we ended up spending a good bit of time together. I also became good friends with my

"Masa Mara Balloon" by Betty Wing (used with permission). Masa Mara Plain, Kenya. 2017

fellow waitress, a Lebanese woman who'd married an Israeli. She'd come to the United States to work while he served in the Israeli Army.

Similar situational friendships have carried us through many trips. A week on an Amazon cruise with an English couple who had such a dim view of people from our country that they were surprised to find Americans they liked. Several days wandering around beautiful Prague with a good-humored couple from Massachusetts. If we hadn't ventured an acquaintance with a shipping executive from Rotterdam and his physician wife in Zambia, we would never have joined them on a fantastic helicopter tour over Victoria Falls, an excursion that hadn't been in our original plans. In a few instances, we've become buddies on a trip and then never encountered the person again, even though we've shared deep thoughts, excitement over a temple tour, or evenings around the campfire. That's fine; meeting people we're compatible with, even for two weeks or a few days, can expand our horizons. All the better if they're from a different country or region of the United States.

But we've also met people who we've stayed in touch with for years. On our first trip to East Africa, we shared a vehicle for the entire safari with two couples, and the six of us developed an excellent trip friendship. We stayed in touch when we returned home. One couple even arranged for all of us to spend time together a few years later at their home in California. Then we hatched a plan with the California couple to travel to France together. Let's just say the different travel environments—a river cruise and a house rental—revealed less journey compatibility than we'd had on safari. Although we remained in infrequent contact, we never traveled together again.

However, on a subsequent safari in Uganda, our group of ten bonded famously, and we became immediate friends with one couple from Montana. In Steve and Betty Wing, Mike and I found perfect travel partners and lifetime friends. We've visited each other's homes multiple times and have taken many subsequent trips together. In turn, Betty and Steve introduced us to another Montana couple, Kathy and Mike Sehestedt, who joined us on a southern African safari. And now, the six of us travel together from time to time.

Mike and I still like to travel on our own, too, especially when we're going someplace to relax and recharge or recapture old memories. And, even the best travel companions have different priority destinations, schedules, and travel commitments that lead to divergent paths in any given year.

Though travel companions can enhance a trip, they can also provide unexpected—and sometimes cringeworthy—moments. In a group tour or a cruise, we might receive the names of our traveling companions in advance, but we really have no idea who we'll be traveling with until we meet them at our destination. Since nearly all our prepackaged tours are small (twenty or fewer people), we usually get to know the entire group. For the most part, the trips we choose are considered adventure travel. The others on the tours are generally frequent travelers, there for many of the same reasons we are. But even frequent travelers run the gamut from wonderful folks we love to hang out with to the occasional boor we try to avoid for the entire trip. I suppose we should count ourselves fortunate that we've never encountered a traveling companion so dangerous as those who are a staple in suspense and mystery novels. Our companions have never involved us in murder and mayhem like Hitchcock's classic *Strangers on a Train*, Christie's *Murder on the Orient Express,* or Highsmith's *The Talented Mr. Ripley.* Nonetheless, we've had a few uncomfortable, if less lethal, fellow travelers.

On one of our trips to Southeast Asia, only three other people joined the tour. A middle-aged couple and a widow traveling on her own. He was a recently divorced attorney; she was his office manager. The widow was a lovely woman, a frequent traveler who decided that she would vacation on her own, if necessary, after her husband's death. She spent most of her free time with Mike and me as we tried to avoid the other couple. We've all run across some version of the male half of the pair somewhere. To hear him (again and again and again), he was a very prominent person in their small town and thought that entitled him to special treatment, even in the remote backcountry of Laos. His girlfriend seemed one of those needy people who wore clothes much too fancy for activities like floating down the Mekong in longboats. They routinely found their room for the night, whether upscale urban hotel or rustic lodge, lacking.

Our most embarrassing—and potentially dangerous—moment with this couple-from-hell came in Communist Vietnam. We were visiting the simple Stilt House where former leader Ho Chi Minh lived during the Vietnam War and the rest of his tenure in office. Heavily armed Vietnamese soldiers guarded both the house and the rest of the Presidential Palace compound. As our young native guide briefed us about Ho Chi Minh and his home, the attorney began a loud rant against Ho Chi Minh and Communism.

Our guide tried to quiet the lawyer and edged us away from the soldiers. The genuinely frightened young man pleaded, "Please, sir. Talk like this is not permitted. If they hear your criticism, the guards could arrest me. I could lose my guide license. This compound is a sacred place, revered by the Party faithful."

The arrogant lawyer brushed off our guide's words of caution and continued to rail against Communism. Exasperated, Mike, the widow, and I stepped in and yelled at the blowhard to shut up.

"Be quiet. Listen to our guide."

"You're going to get us all arrested."

"Stop. Just Stop."

Our concerted efforts finally got through to the lawyer, who shuffled away, mumbling to his girlfriend in pique.

As travelers, we can despise the form of government of the country we're visiting, but it's unwise to loudly criticize that government when surrounded by armed military. And it's particularly unconscionable to risk a local guide's license and personal freedom in doing so. When outside our home country, the very nature of travel means we've entered another nation with its own rules and laws about behavior, including freedom of speech. Those unaware of that fact could find themselves in serious trouble.

This obnoxious attorney is not the only example of Ugly American we've encountered in our travels. All too many exist outside the pages of Graham Greene's novel by that name. Believe me, other nationalities have their own quirks on the road, many of which can pose difficulties. But we've seen a small percentage of Americans who are loud, act entitled, and don't seem to understand that when in another country—whether most developed or least—they're not in Dallas or Akron or Seattle anymore. The sad part is that these jerks give the rest of us American travelers a bad name. For those who watch HGTV's *House Hunters International,* where people rent or buy houses in countries outside their own, you know what I mean. Nothing drives me crazier than when the person who's just talked about how much they're looking forward to the exotic experience of living in <insert foreign country> complains in a haughty voice because a house doesn't have the wine fridge and icemaker that they're used to in Las Vegas. Traveling for weeks on a group tour with someone who evidences this level of cultural cluelessness can get both embarrassing and old.

One of the most bizarre travel companion experiences we've had unfolded on a boat cruise through the remote islands of Indonesia. The trip started rough, literally. The first night on the boat, we encountered very turbulent seas. One couple from our group of twenty passengers disembarked after the first night. The motion of the rustic boat was too difficult for the wife with mobility issues to navigate, so they bailed at the first island we passed.

Another passenger, a single man in his fifties traveling on his own, seemed a little lost in the early days of the cruise. He kept attaching himself to different groups of passengers, trying to make friends. Not surprising in itself. However, midway into the trip, as people chatted, we discovered that Single Guy was telling everyone a different story about his background. He was a *National Geographic* photographer on assignment. He was an FBI agent. He was a novelist. We never actually found out which, if any, of the stories were true.

However, a few days into the voyage, Single Guy annoyed an older gentleman in his eighties who walked with a cane. The older man reminded me a bit of the attorney in Vietnam. He proclaimed, loudly and often, that he owned a manufacturing business and was Very. Well. Off. The older man and the FBI Agent/Photographer/Novelist had a few words one night at dinner, which the older man's wife quickly smoothed over. Things calmed down for several days. That changed when we reached our farthest destination, Rinca Island, one of just four islands inhabited by the dangerous Komodo dragons.

In the pre-briefing for the Komodo dragons visit, our guides warned us to remain very quiet around the giant lizards. They said that we'd see a big group of mature dragons at the ranger station and should avoid making loud noises or startling the beasts while we observed them. Of course, as we stood near these giant lizards that can kill someone with a single drop of their venom, the older man ignored the quiet rule started to talk in a Very. Loud. Voice. The single guy told him to "hush." While not an unreasonable request, his tone was a bit abrasive.

A few hours later, we all stood on the floating docks, waiting to board the dinghies back to our boat. That's when the older man, offended by the earlier shushing, started yelling at Single Guy and then whacked him with his cane. The younger guy, perhaps using his alleged FBI training, reacted by punching the older man, who wobbled but stayed on his feet. The exasperated guides pulled them apart as if separating unruly toddlers on the playground. The fact that this entire escapade took place in front of a boatload of riveted Japanese tourists mortified the rest of our group. Luckily, the two combatants stayed far apart for the sail back to Bali.

Even traveling on our own, we've been negatively affected by people encountered along the way. Barely avoiding getting knocked out by a selfie stick held by a tourist jostling to get that perfect photo of his own face in front of stunning Yellowstone Falls. Trying to get that shot of the Taj Mahal or other famous monument without a crowd of strangers in the picture. Missing out on those pancakes I was eyeing at the breakfast buffet in the Dominican Republic because the glutton in front of me walks away with the entire tray for her family. Yes, the whole tray.

Just as often, we've shared a bonding moment with fellow travelers who happened to be at the same place at the same time. Recently, we arrived at Bryce Canyon's Sunset Point to find that the sunset included a spectacular rainbow. We shared the magic moment with a young couple on bicycles and a park ranger, as we all—even the ranger—oohed and awed at the beautiful show nature had offered. Or, on our first safari in Kenya, all of those returning from our game drives one night had to make a rather frightening crossing of a suspension footbridge over a river gorge to get into camp. The regular entrance was temporarily closed for reasons I've now forgotten. When everyone had successfully made it across the bridge, camp staff welcomed us with drinks served around the campfire. We continued our group bonding experience by sharing the stories of how each of the couples there had met. After an hour and a half of navigating a hanging bridge by flashlight and exchanging personal information, it felt like we'd known these total strangers for years.

I regard these moments of joy shared with strangers, people we'll never see again, as a testament to the fact that much more binds us together in life than separates us, no matter our country or life experiences. Such gratifying moments more than offset the exasperating ones.

Our most hair-raising interaction with temporary travel companions came on a small airplane flight (twentyish seats) to view Mt. Everest in Nepal. Mike and I, along with a young couple from Argentina, were sandwiched onto a plane with a Chinese tour group. Once in the air, the flight attendant explained over the audio system that the pilot would fly along the mountain range, then past Mt. Everest. So that everyone would have a good view of the world's highest peak, the plane would make a loop, with all passengers getting the full mountain profile on either the outbound flight or the return trip.

As we approached the legendary peak on the first pass, all the Chinese tourists on the far side of the plane leaped into the aisle to peer through the windows at Everest. One woman even hopped into Mike's lap. The plane canted to the left as the pilot tried to manage the abrupt shift of all that weight onto one side. Yelling to be heard over the commotion, the flight attendant ran up and down the aisle, frantically wrestling the small-framed travelers back into their seats.

With everyone settled in their proper places, the flight attendant announced that, one by one, each passenger could now go forward into the cockpit and see the mountain from a pilot's-eye view.

That's when all the Chinese tourists again jumped up and tried to flood the cockpit. As the plane wobbled, the flight attendant screamed, "Return to your seats immediately" to get their attention. After repeating her command several times in several languages, everyone took their places once again. With that effort, she was able to bring some calm and give us each, in turn, a glimpse at the impressive mountain.

"Okay, one by one, please," the attendant said in a soothing voice as she ushered each passenger into the cockpit in an orderly fashion.

On the return trip, the Chinese group seemed to get the idea that they were to stay seated, so that part of the flight was uneventful. Everest was magnificent, but it could have been a smoother ride. A few years later, I read the terrible news that an Everest flight-seeing plane from the same airline had crashed with all onboard killed. My immediate thought, *it had been downed by excited and unruly tourists*, was incorrect, as the investigation determined that the crash was weather-related.

In discussing travel companions, I'd be remiss if I didn't mention the value that having an excellent local guide can bring to a trip. Of course, if we're going to spend our time on a Caribbean beach or wandering the vineyards of Provence, we don't need assistance. But we've benefitted from having a guide on small group tours, day tours, and even private trips. Guides not only help organize the many details of traveling but also speak the language and have extensive local knowledge to share. One of the less obvious benefits, guides can also describe their lives and help paint a picture of daily life in their country. One of our guides in Uganda took Mike and me to his childhood home and shared some stories about his life as a very young soldier fighting against Joseph Kony's Lord's Resistance Army of child soldiers. Our private group guide on a month-long safari in Botswana proved a great background resource for one of my novels, *Dead on the Delta,* as he provided a wealth of information about wildlife and the country. A guide in Iceland drove off the main route to show us some lesser-seen aspects of the island's geothermal power system. He also gave us the rundown on the public swimming pools available to both locals and visitors alike.

Guides can provide a personal perspective on local customs and history. A young local guide in one of the tiger reserves in Madya Pradesh gave us insight into how tough it is for women to break into the male-dominated profession of wildlife guide in India. The guide who drove our black taxi through Belfast, Northern Ireland, spoke about his time in the Irish Republican Army and recounted his childhood memory of the bombing of his neighborhood around Bombay Street. This incident ignited the decades-long "troubles" between Irish Catholics and Protestants.

Our private guide in India shared a lot about his family and his life in Madhya Pradesh. When COVID flared out of control in India, I reached out to Narendra to make sure that he and his family were well. The young PhD candidate who guided us through Myanmar plied us with Burmese history and anecdotes of his childhood. I now worry about Daniel's future under the steadily more restrictive military regime that's cracking down on democracy in Myanmar.

One of our most memorable, if short-lived, guides drove our bus on a day trip into Denali National Park. She wheeled that vehicle, a beat-up, repurposed school bus, across the park, pointing out key sights, spotting elk, moose, and grizzlies, all the while keeping up a nonstop narrative about her life as a homesteader in Alaska. The guide and her family lived in a remote cabin year-round, miles from the nearest town. During the short summer months, she'd earn money by driving this tour through Denali. But, otherwise, she and her husband lived off the land and off the grid, making it through long, dark, snowy winters on their own, trapping and hunting to survive. Although her tales were fascinating, they made me realize how hard life as a modern-day Jeremiah Johnson could be in a state where winter days bring only a few hours of light, and in summer, the sun can shine all night long.

Bottom line, the companions we've traveled with and travelers met along the way have enriched our experiences. Even when some people annoyed us or made the trip more difficult, they often provided valuable lessons on how not to behave. More often, we've expanded our horizons by learning from travelers and guides about different countries, cultures, and perspectives on the world. Although I'm more of an introvert, I've become more comfortable reaching out to strangers when traveling over the years. As a result, I've learned that one key to interesting travel is to engage with those I meet along the way.

Tips for Travelers

I N ONE key way, travel resembles life itself. The farther we venture down the path, the more we learn. Mike and I have traveled enough that we've picked up a few approaches that make our life easier while on the road. We've developed most of these tips as the result of experience, not all of it positive. Sometimes bad experiences can prove the best teachers.

Note that these are ideas, techniques, and suggestions that work for us. Everyone has their own style, preferences, likes, and dislikes, so they may not work for all. With those caveats, here are a few travel tips. I may have mentioned some of them in previous chapters, and I'm sharing them in no order of importance. Although I've written these tips from my perspective as a US citizen, most can easily adapt to other countries of residence.

1. When flying to a destination, **ARRIVE A DAY EARLY** if you can—especially when crossing multiple time zones. A free day before your scheduled activities begin allows you to adjust to the time, the climate, catch up on any lost sleep, and make sure your luggage arrives. Building an extra day into your itinerary also provides a hedge against delayed or canceled flights.

2. Before you leave, **TAKE PHOTOS OF YOUR LUGGAGE**, and make sure you pack all your essentials and a change in clothes appropriate to your first stop in your carry-on bag. We learned that lesson when our luggage went astray on an Air Italia flight to Italy. We spent three days shivering in our Tuscan villa because all our warmer clothes

"Okavango Waterlily" by Mike Knowlton. Okavango Delta, Botswana. 2010

were in those checked bags. That early lesson was reinforced when a couple traveling on our cruise down the Amazon arrived at the port, but their luggage didn't. They wore the clothes they traveled in for two days until the airline located their suitcases and ferried them to the riverboat via a speedboat that tracked us down while in passage.

3. **CARRY A FLASHLIGHT** and wrap duct tape around the handle. A flashlight comes in handy if there are power outages, to help navigate dark corridors or streets, or to just find your way to the bathroom in a strange room at night. We've found duct tape to be invaluable for everything from patching torn suitcases to a temporary repair of a ripped pant seam to plucking cell phones from the tundra under the watchful eye of a polar bear. (More on this story in Volume 2 of my travel memoir: *Beyond the Sunset: Expanding My Horizons*.)

4. **PACK LIGHT.** And, when you believe that you've packed as light as humanly possible to survive the trip, go through your suitcase and take a few more things out. Unless you're a model or a movie star who will be photographed wherever you go, most of the people you'll encounter while traveling will never see you again. The guy you meet at a café in Brussels will have no idea you wore the same dress at the Louvre two days ago. The *maître d'* at that fancy restaurant only cares that you meet the dress code and has no idea you wore the same jacket last night. Even if you're traveling with a tour group, the women are all too busy worrying if anyone noticed they're wearing that blue blouse for the fifth time to pay attention to your outfit. And the men, who are wearing the exact same clothes for the fourteenth day in a row, will notice nothing at all about your apparel.

5. **DON'T WEAR OR BRING A LOT OF VALUABLES**, especially to countries with socioeconomic challenges. If you're taking a high-end trip to a world-renowned city or resort where everyone will be dressed to the nines, perhaps nice jewelry and designer clothes are *de rigeur*. But, on adventure trips, African safaris, and even most package tours, you don't want to risk losing that expensive ring, watch, or diamond earrings. And in many places in the world we've traveled, a piece of jewelry, electronics, or a designer bag can be worth more than

a typical family makes in an entire year. Poverty can lead to crime. Why encourage theft by flaunting expensive items or stacks of cash?

6. **TRY TO BLEND IN**. I realize this one might be controversial, but Mike and I try not to parade around the world looking like the stereotypical American. We've found that Americans, in general, are easily identifiable in many ways, both big and small, by our clothing, our mannerisms, our inability to speak other languages, our straight teeth, our tendency to smile all the time. But the countries that we visit have their own customs, religious traditions, political environments, and tolerance for outsiders. Learning a little about those unique practices and deferring to those traditions, even if it makes you wince, can make your trip smoother. And, if part of travel is learning what makes people in other countries and regions tick, why wouldn't you offer that modicum of respect to your hosts? I believe most Americans would expect outsiders to respect our customs when traveling through the United States, right?

Accommodations to blend in can be minor, like not wearing white sneakers or shirts proclaiming your home team. In Italy, churches ask women to cover their heads with a scarf and both sexes to wear pants/skirts that cover the knee. Other countries with a conservative religious tradition frown upon swimwear outside hotels and beaches. In places with a Muslim population, like the Kenyan island of Lamu, photographing women's faces is prohibited. In many more countries, photographing soldiers or military installations can lead to jail time. So, while some of the blending-in and following-the-rules processes can simply be courtesy, they can prevent criminal charges in extreme cases.

Other times, like on safari, blending in can mean wearing neutral clothing that won't attract the attention of wild animals. Those shades can also help disguise the constant dust. Or the advisory to not wear blue in some safari spots can help you avoid tsetse flies, their painful bites, and the illness that some may carry.

7. **LEARN SOME BASIC PHRASES IN THE LANGUAGE**. I studied French in high school and college, and Mike, Spanish, although neither of us approach any type of fluency. Those two are the only languages other

than English with which we have any real familiarity—except for a few phrases of German picked up from watching World War II movies. As a Romance language, Italian shares some similarities with French and Spanish. That can help us decipher signs, at least.

We've found that even our attempts at rusty and likely grammatically incorrect French and Spanish can go a long way toward breaking the ice in French- and Spanish-speaking countries. Most people are pleased that we made an effort before they rescue us and continue the conversation in their often-perfect English. However, with older people or in more remote areas, that smattering of French and Spanish is what gets us through a halting conversation with people who only speak their native language.

In non-English speaking countries, we always try to learn some of the most basic phrases that combine courtesy and practical necessity. These include *Hello. Goodbye. Please. Thank you. Excuse me. Help. Where is the toilet? How much does this cost?*

Without these essential phrases, a traveler is utterly reliant on either guides, the limited usefulness of a cell-phone language app, or a local who speaks English. Many countries in the world require students to learn English from an early age, but not everyone does, especially in remote areas. And we've found many people who are not confident in using the English they do know. The language dilemma becomes even more complicated in countries that use an alphabet other than Latin. In countries such as Greece, India, Nepal, and those across Asia, it's easy to feel adrift and confused when signs, menus, and more use symbols with which a native-English speaker is unfamiliar. Learning the phonetic pronunciations of these essentials, along with the name of your hotel (and carrying your hotel name on a card written in the local script), can be lifesavers.

8. Before leaving home, **PREPARE A CURRENCY CONVERSION CHART.** I type up a little card to carry or you could put a note on your cell phone that lists four or five dollar amounts and their conversion into the currency of each country you're visiting. For example, $1 = X Euros, $5 = Y Euros, $10 = Z Euros. We've found that a written conversion chart is an easy way to orient ourselves when making a

purchase or planning a currency exchange. For me, it's easier than doing the exchange rate multiplication in my head or using an app on my phone. It's particularly helpful when dealing with a currency in which each unit is worth significantly less or more than the dollar, i.e., 1 US dollar is worth 14,476 Indonesian rupiahs (at the tim eof this writing). Having a little cheat sheet can also be helpful if traveling from one country to the next where each uses a different currency. Just as I've memorized the conversion rate in the first country, we move on and must start all over again. It can get especially confusing as the number of countries we enter expands. I find that having the cheat sheet makes the transition so much easier.

9. **LET PEOPLE KNOW WHERE YOU'RE GOING.** Register your itinerary with the US State Department before you leave. It's a crazy world out there, and unexpected events can happen. Terrorist attacks, natural disasters like floods or earthquakes, labor strikes that shut down an airport or borders, an outbreak of war, or border conflict. If you go online and register your itinerary with the State Department, that means someone from the US government knows you're in an affected country and roughly where you might be. Generally, the US government tries to assist US citizens in the wake of serious events, getting them out of the country when indicated. Filling out the form takes just a few minutes and could help with your rescue if the worst happens. We register with the State Department on all our foreign trips.

Similarly, leave a copy of your scheduled flights and your trip itinerary, including an emergency number for your cruise line, travel company, etc., with a family member or close friend when you're traveling. In cases of natural disasters, accidents, and more, it's rarely enough for your family member to know that you were flying to France on Tuesday. Providing them in advance with information on airline, airport, flight, and itinerary can help alleviate a lot of unnecessary anxiety or, conversely, let family members know that you might be in trouble.

10. **TAKE THE PROPER HEALTH PRECAUTIONS** before and during the trip. If you're visiting a less-developed country, book an appointment with your doctor or a travel clinic to ensure you are appropriately

immunized and have any necessary medication. Certain immunizations must be administered in a series, so check with the clinic to determine how far in advance to schedule the appointment. If you won't have ready access to doctors and pharmacies, pack a few basic over-the-counter medications as well as an extended supply of your prescription medications in your carry-on bag. Know in advance whether the water is safe to drink at your destination and know which foods, if any, the CDC recommends you avoid. That includes checking CDC recommendations for activities to avoid in the country of your destination. These things can range from traveling at night to special advisories regarding unprotected sex or rape to the dangers of swimming in certain local bodies of water.

The common theme for all these tips is: Be prepared. I always depart hoping a trip is incident- and illness-free. Some of these travel tips can help ensure that everything goes smoothly. The others can help make it easier to deal with an unexpected situation.

'On the Trail 1974' by Mike Knowlton. Sherry Knowlton in Rocky Mountain National Park, Colorado. 1974

Leaving the Comfort Zone Behind

REJOICE THAT I live in an era when travel to even the remotest spot on the globe is usually possible. Most of the places I've dreamed about seeing, many since my youth, are easily accessible or options exist for reaching them. When Mike and I retired (in my case, semi-retired) and had the luxury of free time, we leaped into international travel with a vengeance. We made a deliberate decision when we stopped full-time work in our late fifties that we would start with the more strenuous and exotic trips first and ease into the accessible and sedate destinations and modes of travel as we age.

That meant African safaris and elephant riding in Laos sooner than leisurely barge cruises through Provence. The mix hasn't been quite as definitive as we originally outlined, but we have checked off many of the most remote destinations from our evolving wish list. At the same time, we've sneaked in a smattering of relaxing river cruises and European trips between weeks of bumpy, dust-filled tiger safaris in India and challenging hikes in Patagonia. All in all, that decision has served us well.

I abhor that over-used phrase "Bucket List." Perhaps I prefer not to face my mortality and the concept of "kicking the bucket," from which the term derives. I also dislike it because Bucket List implies that, at a point in time, everyone throws a definitive list of places to go and things to do into a pail. And that this list of locations and experiences falls to the bottom of the pail and can only be plucked out and discarded upon completion.

Mike and I view our joint wish list as both evolving and subject to frequent edit. Okay. Usually, the revisions involve adding new destinations. Mike or I will read about a place or see a movie filmed in a particular location, and we'll say, "Let's go there." However, other spots move up and down on the list based on our changing interest or when a new place for various reasons, sometimes intangible, becomes a "must-see." Others may sink out of sight forever.

Let's face it. My worldview as a child was limited. When I read a book or otherwise learned about a destination, some wormed their way deep into my heart. The Rocky Mountains, Greece, Paris, a safari in Africa—I internalized these as places I must absolutely visit someday. And now I have. Other areas may have sounded intriguing, but the compulsion to visit didn't occupy my heart and dreams. Since those childhood days, I've learned about many more spots to explore in the world and developed a fuller picture of some of those intriguing but no longer quite as compelling destinations. So, my "must-see" list has evolved.

We've also visited places that never made our wish list. A few times, we've embarked on a journey simply because friends have said, "We're going to X in the spring. Want to come along?" We've discovered some great destinations that way, whether it's the polar bear migration onto Hudson Bay in Churchill, Manitoba, or a little hotel in the British Virgin Islands called the Sugar Mill.

Other times, a place I've wanted to see for years unexpectedly loses its appeal. Sometimes geopolitics and the situation on the ground make a destination less desirable or downright unsafe. In other instances, my enthusiasm dims for reasons even I don't fully understand. For example, I'd always wanted to see the pyramids of Egypt and cruise the Nile on a *felucca*. But the political situation became volatile there for several years, followed by a spate of tourist bombings. So, even though the country has experienced subsequent periods of relative calm and safety, I've lost my enthusiasm for seeing the Sphinx by moonlight. Another country once high on my wish list, Australia, no longer excites me. Even I am not entirely clear why. But, if I ever get there, it will likely be as an add-on to a return to New Zealand, which I absolutely loved. Heaven on earth.

I often ponder how travel has changed over the centuries. I suppose there have always been nomadic people who roam their own region or the larger world with just the few supplies they can transport by foot, camel, or outrigger canoe. Think of Deerslayer, Uncas, and Chingach-gook walking miles through the Adirondack forests in *The Last of the Mohicans,* or the Western trapper played by Robert Redford in the movie *Jeremiah Johnson* slogging through the snow of the Rockies.

But, for every tale of resilient people who journeyed through the world, spare and stripped down to the essentials, living off the land, there is another story of mind-blowing excess. Teddy Roosevelt's *African Game Trails* chronicles his 1904 safari from East Africa to the Belgian Congo to Khartoum with an entourage of two hundred fifty guides and porters carrying vast amounts of luggage and equipment. Teddy, the brash, self-promoting swashbuckler, is among my favorite presidents if for no other reason than he created the national park system. But, really, Teddy? A support team of two hundred fifty?

Roosevelt's approach to a big game safari or wilderness exploration wasn't unique for adventurers of the day. In 1871, reporter Henry Morton Stanley assembled a caravan of one hundred porters when he struck out across the African continent on his search for the missing explorer David Livingstone. When the rescue mission found Livingstone in what is now Tanzania, they'd traveled seven hundred miles overland.

Of course, wilderness travelers in those days didn't have motorized vehicles, paved roads, supply chains, GPS, and satellite cell phones with full internet capabilities. So, their version of Be Prepared involved bringing a wide range of contingency items in tow by necessity. Still, the locals must have been, by turns, appalled or amused by what these explorers regarded as the travel essentials.

These famous explorers of Western civilization are joined in history by others who sought to know what lies beyond the horizon. Some, like Hannibal, sought to conquer new worlds. Some, like Marco Polo, sought to expand trade and get rich. Still others as diverse as the Crusaders, the Moors, and Catholic missionaries sought to export their version of God to new regions. The Vikings and the Polynesians are famous for sailing far beyond their homes. The Romans conquered France and Britain. The Spanish and Portuguese sent ships to explore the New World across the Atlantic. Some anthropologists believe that the first humans evolved in Africa and spread out by foot over connected continents to eventually populate all the other major landmasses. So, the urge to seek out new places and new adventures is endemic to human nature.

However, these hardy travelers were often the exception. For centuries, most people never saw the world beyond a day's walk from their homes. Other than soldiers and sailors, few ventured beyond their own country. When adventurers set sail on the ocean or found their way to another continent, the trips took months or, more often, years. In contrast, today, we can board an airplane in New York City and disembark fourteen hours later in Beijing. Even trips to the farthest reaches of the world that involve multiple modes of transportation can take just a few days. A hardy nature may be a plus for travel in the modern world, but it's rarely essential.

I won't pretend that travel doesn't cost money. But when Mike and I started to travel in our early twenties—and for quite a while afterward—we managed on a shoestring budget. We stayed in campgrounds and those little cabin motels we found along the road and in many tourist spots. Hard to believe that when we started our travels, we could stay in national forest campgrounds that cost a dollar a night. Many operated on the honor system, so we just slipped our payment into a box at the entrance. Since we often traveled in the early fall, we sometimes had a campground entirely to ourselves. We cooked over campfires and camp stoves or in cabin kitchenettes. Restaurants were a luxury. But the most important thing to Mike and me was the journey, not the lodging or fancy meals. And we made those hiking trips and, later, trips to the Caribbean a priority in our limited budget.

Although hardly in the Teddy Roosevelt sphere of excess, I relish some comforts when I travel these days. And, in our retirement, we can better afford those comforts. My enthusiasm for sleeping on the ground and cooking over a campfire has waned. Roughing it can still be fun in small doses on a trip, but only if balanced with a few days of lodging with comfy beds and prepared meals.

Another common way to travel with little money is to find jobs in the places you want to visit. All over the world, we've met people who wanted to experience an area of the world, so they moved there to work. Often those have been young people who find jobs in the tourist industry, like waiting on tables or guiding river rafting tours. But we've met people of all ages who've found temporary work the best way to explore new places. Campground hosts who live the season in a state park. Seasonal rangers in the national parks—one was eighty-plus years old! A bus driver in Denali National Park. People who volunteer for the Peace Corps or the various nongovernmental organizations that do good all over the world.

We've found a pattern among many people that involves following the tourist season, i.e., spending the summer in Alaska or Maine and the winter in Hawaii or the Caribbean. Seeing the world can be possible on a limited budget for people who unleash their imaginations and prioritize travel.

Mike and I chose another way to realize our travel dreams. After that multi-month sojourn around the country in our youth, we held full-time jobs at home in Pennsylvania and traveled almost every vacation. We were never ones to "save up" our vacation days in case we needed them for an emergency. Nope. A week or two weeks off? We hit the road or flew to an island. For us, working became the vehicle to fund the vacations.

Don't get me wrong. During our working years, our time for travel was limited by both budget and available vacation days. And, when Josh arrived on the scene, he immediately came first in our lives. We took more traditional family vacations while our son was young, and then the definition of "kid-friendly" grew as Josh did. We funded all these trips with our salaries, designating certain amounts of money for travel. As Mike and I moved up the ladder in our careers, we had more disposable income. Although we had daily living and then our son's college costs, we always prioritized saving money to pay for our trips. But that strategy changed dramatically when we retired. Mike and I suddenly had access to carefully planned retirement savings and extensive time for—yes, exactly—travel. Seeing the world.

And we've reaped the rewards of that travel in so many ways that have enriched our lives. Travel has enhanced my writing and has fostered artistic creativity through photography for both Mike and me. But travel has shaped me in many other ways.

I believe I have a broader approach to life, in general, due to travel. Because I've seen so many different places, cultures, living situations, and economic conditions with my own eyes, because I've met so many varied people who speak other languages and look at life from unique cultural, religious, and geographic perspectives, I better understand the complexity of the world and its political and geopolitical issues. When I read about an earthquake in Nepal, a terrorist bombing in Kenya, a military takeover in Myanmar, or a mass elephant die-off in Botswana, I can better visualize where it happened, understand the impact, and think about people I met whom the incident will affect. Empathy doesn't require a personal connection, but a degree of familiarity with a place or situation can undoubtedly enhance the ability to relate.

My travels have taught me that, in the fundamentals, people across the globe are more similar than different. They go about their daily routines, concerned about making a living, providing a home, feeding and nurturing their families. Most have hopes and dreams for themselves and their children. In every society, there are good people and bad; saints and criminals; inspirational leaders and would-be tyrants. Learning these lessons has provided me with an antidote to the insidious fear of "the other," which is so prevalent now in some segments of the US population and elsewhere. Often, it's those who've never met any kind of "other" who are the most fearful. What a shame.

One of the best things about our travel is how it continues to bring Mike and me closer. When we're home, we spend time together, of course. But we each have our own interests and pursuits. However, when we travel, we're together almost twenty-four hours a day, and the journey creates a time for us to reconnect, to face new experiences and challenges together. I always look forward to the extended one-on-one time with my husband. Since we first met, travel has been an essential part of our lives. Thirst for new adventures has been the warp, and each new trip is the weft that has woven the fabric of our fifty years together. I expect the cloth will only become richer and stronger as we continue to roam the world for as long as possible.

So many of my favorite memories involve travel, and the best involve Mike. Seeing starfish for the first time on an Oregon beach, hiking through the golden glory of Colorado's quaking aspens whispering in the autumn breeze, crawling out of our tent in Maine to a forest covered in early autumn snow, chasing giant shadows at sunset on Botswana's salt flats, sharing a quiet lunch in a warm café on a dreary day in Reykjavik—countless moments of shared joy. Many more of my best memories fill this book. And I intend to build new memories as we continue to explore. I'm so happy that Josh, Laura, and our granddaughters, Julia and Mia, have become essential to our travel memory scrapbook. I look forward to building new memories with them all over the globe.

I thought about ending this book with something predictable like, "When I was that small girl, reading those books about adventures in faraway places, little could I have imagined that one day, I would actually be there." But then, I realized that such a statement is nonsense. The very fact that I could and did imagine myself in all those faraway places is why I eventually reached many of them. Even as a small child, I had a strong will and determination to move beyond my small-town life, my "comfort zone." I met a man who loved the voyage as much as I, and we've relished our periodic odysseys around the world.

Sometimes I envy those people who've embraced travel and adventure in a much more comprehensive way. The couples on television shows who move across the world at the drop of a hat to take a job and live a new life in a foreign city. Scientists, anthropologists, researchers, wildlife photographers, and the like who spend years in remote locations on important projects. The volunteers for Doctors without Borders, the Peace Corps, and other nongovernmental organizations who fly across the globe to help people in need. Those people fully immerse themselves in a new country, a new location, and freefall out of their comfort zones into something entirely unfamiliar. Maybe in my next life.

But in this life, I'm content with my choices. Mike and I have traveled extensively in a way that works for us. And as long as I'm physically able, I'll continue "to travel beyond the sunset and the baths of all the . . . stars"—western, eastern, northern, and southern.

"Shadow Puppets" by Sherry Knowlton. Yogyakarta, Java, Indonesia. 2012

Follow Sherry (and Mike!) around the world in *Volume 2: Beyond the Sunset: A Travel Memoir, Expanding My Horizons* coming in December 2022.

Enjoy the Journey

I DOUBT THAT I'll ever be able to fully answer the chicken-or-the-egg question about why I so love to travel. I know that, from an early age, my love of reading opened my world to the possibilities outside my hometown. As that childhood desire to travel blossomed, a quote from Tennyson's poem *Ulysses* that I posted on a bulletin board in my room became my touchstone:

> ". . . for my purpose holds to sail beyond the sunset, and the baths of all the western stars, until I die . . ."

I now realize that it's also integral to my nature to push the limits and step outside my comfort zone.

Regardless of the origins of my jonesing for travel, fortune smiled upon me when I met my husband, Mike, and found in him a fellow traveler. This second volume of *Beyond the Sunset* continues to chronicle our journeys together through anecdotes and musings about our time exploring the world. In writing these books, I've come to an important realization. While reading and my natural inclination to experience new things and new places were the sparks that set me on the road, being mindful and open to each new travel adventure has truly allowed my passion for travel to ignite and burn with a steady flame. After an extended road trip in my post-college years, Mike and I held increasingly demanding jobs and raised a son, all the while spending as much time traveling as we could. When we retired from full-time work a little over a decade ago, Mike and

I had the freedom to spend more time exploring the world. Throughout our years of hiking, sailing, and traveling to new places, we've had many memorable adventures, met interesting people the world over, and learned much about differences among countries and cultures. We've learned even more about what bonds people together, including universal values like the love of family and the need for a safe living environment. Most of all, these journeys have led me to better understand what makes me tick.

To fully appreciate each journey, I can't be one of those travelers Mike and I have encountered who rush around a city with a list, determined to check off each monument mentioned in the guidebook. Of course, I wanted to see the Taj Mahal, the Eiffel Tower, and the Empire State Building. But I've learned over time that slowing down and leaving space in our trips for sitting, observing, absorbing, and allowing the unexpected to happen can both give me a better feel for the place and often result in some of our most memorable days. When I allow myself that space, I feel less like a tourist passing through and more like a traveler who's assimilating into a new environment—even though our time there may be brief.

Our first time in Paris, Mike and I spent an entire day just wandering. We had a few destinations that we wanted to visit, but mostly we just walked and chose the streets that looked most interesting. We spent time absorbing the calm of Monet's waterlilies at L'Orangerie. We watched several old men play *boules* in the Tuileries Garden. We visited Shakespeare and Company, a place some of my literary heroes haunted in their heydays. We sat for quite a while, having tea and croissants at a sidewalk café. Whiled away another hour-plus, lunching on cheesy *Croque Monsieurs* at another sidewalk café. Poked into a few shops. Took in the fountains and the view from the Trocadero. We chatted with servers, shopkeepers, and fellow travelers, but other times we just listened to the French and other languages swirl around us. Thomas Jefferson said, "A walk about Paris will provide lessons in history, beauty, and in the point of life." I agree. Our meanderings through the famed City of Light allowed us to feel the pavement beneath our feet while absorbing the essence of the city through our senses. Each step we walked merged the Paris of my dreams with the reality I was experiencing and brought me closer to Jefferson's soaring conclusion that the city can help teach the "point of life."

Mike and I have taken similar approaches to cities and small towns from Florence, Chang Mai, and Auckland to tiny, off-the-beaten-track villages in Alaska, New Hampshire, and Laos. We also like to visit many key sights, on our own or through guided tours, but we find that spending time just roaming a city can be the best introduction.

Wandering without a specific plan can work equally well in rural or wilderness environments. On one of our safaris in Tanzania, our guide was driving Mike, Josh, his girlfriend at the time, and me on the Serengeti Plain. Isaac had taken us to several spots that he knew were prime animal viewing locations, including a very active hippo pool. But we hadn't seen any big cats that morning, so we were just meandering through dirt roads not far from our campsite. When we spied two young male elephants jousting, Isaac stopped on a slightly elevated road that overlooked a grassland punctuated by a shallow ravine formed by a small stream. The elephants, part of a larger herd, continued to tussle, practicing for the day that they might have to fight another male in earnest to win a harem. A herd of impala grazed nearby, unconcerned by the elephant shenanigans. While we took photos of the sparring elephants, Isaac noticed a group of four female lions approaching from the far left. They stopped, checked out the impalas, and went into hunting mode, crouching low to the ground. Meanwhile, the elephant boys had tired of their game and rejoined their family.

The female lions edged nearer and nearer to the impala, using clumps of tall grass for cover. Then, in one coordinated move, they streaked over the remaining distance, clearly hoping to bring down an impala for lunch. The spooked herd fled, but one of the lionesses caught a straggling impala and killed it with a snap of her jaws. She and her sisters headed almost directly toward us, making their way toward the ravine, perhaps seeking a protected spot to dine. Out of nowhere, a male lion came tearing across the savanna and bowled over the female as he snatched the impala carcass from her mouth. Although the lion sisters growled and hissed, the male of their pride trotted away to the ravine with the dead impala.

That's when several of the largest female elephants from the herd charged the male lion. According to Isaac, the matriarch and her companions were likely unhappy with the commotion and smell of blood near their babies. So, the elephants rushed the male several times, bugling and stamping their feet. Finally, he dropped the impala carcass and slunk away. Their problem solved, the elephant ladies returned to their children. After a brief wait to make sure the coast was clear, the four lionesses moved back in to reclaim the impala and settled in for a snack. This entire saga played out right in front of us like a live National Geographic special; a perfect illustration of the unexpected moments that have come our way when we wander.

Safaris are a great example of the wander-until-we-stumble-across-something-interesting approach to travel. We had another great moment our first time in the Kalahari Desert. Mike and I were alone with our guide driving to a series of waterholes that remained even during the dry season and thus attracted animals in the area to water. At the first waterhole, we watched quite an assortment of elephants, oryx, and wildebeest as they took turns drinking at the water's edge. When we moved onto the next waterhole bordered by a small grove of trees, we happened upon a unique situation. Set up beneath the shade of the branches, a vet was treating a sick lion. At the edge of the pool, partially submerged, lay the carcass of a brown hyena. (The elusive and rare brown hyena has a much smaller range and longer fur than the more common spotted hyena.) As the vet worked on the unconscious male lion, which had been darted with sedatives, he told us that the hyena died from poison. He didn't know the origin of the poison. He suspected that the lion had come upon the dying or dead hyena and had eaten some of the carcass or drunk the tainted water. So, he was treating the lion for poisoning. We stayed and watched him take the lion's temperature and administer several injections. When the lion started to stir, the vet asked us to leave before the animal awoke—to lessen distraction and stress as the animal regained consciousness. Imagine being a vet who makes "house calls" to sickly lions in the remote desert!

Another way to help absorb a new place comes with tuning into the arts and culture of a country. Music, dance, museums, street art, handicrafts, and more can be ways to learn about the place we're visiting. We always wander through craft markets, sometimes buy "tourist" art from sidewalk artists, and often stop to take in performances by street musicians or local celebrations that we pass. Near Ranthambore park in Rajasthan, India, we drove past a wedding ceremony. A crowd of guests stood in the street, toasting the bride and groom. When our guide slowed down to a near stop, the revelers turned, shot streamers in the air toward us, and for a few brief moments embraced us in their happy celebration.

In South Africa, we were on a guided walking tour of Soweto, a largely slum suburb of Johannesburg. At the end of the tour, we returned to our car, which was parked near a large plaza. Several young men asked our guide if they could sing for us. They performed an a cappella trio of songs, including the South African national anthem, in a small building displaying local tourist information. The hollow concrete structure amplified their voices; the singing was truly beautiful. Of course, the young men perform primarily to earn money, but their joy in the songs shone in their intricate harmonies.

Another type of performance that I've learned to seek out on trips is puppet shows. Three different shows we've seen stand out in my memory. In Vietnam, we took in a water puppet show at the Thang Long Theater in Hanoi. The elaborate production included live musicians and singers who provided the background music for the puppet show, which took place on a pool of water. The twelve-to-forty-inch puppets were handled on bamboo rods and strings by a group of puppeteers hidden behind a pagoda with bamboo screens.

That show differed in both pageantry and expertise from a charming puppet show we watched at our hotel in Madhya Pradesh, India. A father and two young sons, dressed in lavish embroidered clothes and turbans, staged the performance. The father operated the colorful puppets, and the boys provided a soundtrack with an accordion and traditional drums. The show had an amateurish feel that I found charming, especially when the youngest boy flubbed the drumbeat at a crucial scene in the play.

My absolute favorite puppetry is the much more basic shadow puppetry of Java, Indonesia. I'd always wanted to see shadow puppets ever since I'd watched the 1982 movie *The Year of Living Dangerously*, based on the novel of the same name by Christopher Koch. The movie focuses on the violent times surrounding the end of the Sukarno regime in the mid-1960s. Shadow puppets appeared only briefly in one scene, but I fell for the exotic atmosphere of Indonesia painted in the movie and, especially, for the shadow puppets. I was thrilled to see a shadow puppet show one afternoon in Java. Elaborately carved flat leather puppets are attached to bamboo sticks. Stationed behind a barely opaque cloth screen, the puppet master moves the puppets to act out the story described in music and song. Usually, the story follows the plot and stylized conventions of the Hindu epic, the *Ramayana*. The audience sits on the opposite side of the screen and sees only the silhouettes of the puppets, which are lit from behind. The shadows projected by the backlit puppets can look like they're running, walking, or dancing. I was entranced by the ornate craftsmanship of the two-dimensional puppets, the mystery of a tale told in light and shadow, and the simple mechanics of the production. We later got a chance to view the puppets from the other side of the screen—a further peek into the mystery of these traditional productions.

In Yogyakarta, we also saw the *Ramayana* performed as a ballet on an outdoor stage at night with the ancient Prambanan Temples in the background. The elaborate costumes and ritualized dancing of the Indonesian version of the Hindu epic lived up to the exoticism promised by *The Year of Living Dangerously*. From James Hilton's *Lost Horizon* to James Clavell's *Shogun,* many novels have romanticized the notion of westerners succumbing to the lure of the Far East. I can attest that the contrast in East/West cultures can seduce a traveler.

Music and dance provide a window into cultures everywhere. I find value even in those performances tailored primarily to tourists. Yes, sometimes the dance I'm watching or the music I'm hearing might not represent how the average family in the country spends their time on Saturday nights. But that doesn't lessen the importance of that dance or music in the history and the culture of the country or region. The demand for tourist performances often helps keep traditional art alive, both in foreign lands and in my home country.

At the Crazy Horse Monument in South Dakota, we watched a troupe of Native Americans perform a series of tribal dances. Seeing these men and young boys in tribal dress go through a series of steps passed down through their tribe for centuries embodied the massive cultural preservation effort that sponsored their dance. In the late 1940s, Lakota Chief Henry Standing Bear enlisted sculptor Korczak Ziolkowski to carve a tribute to famous Lakota Chief Crazy Horse from a mountain in the Black Hills, a place sacred to Native Americans. When I first saw the work in progress, I was impressed by the size and the vision inherent in such a project. (Think: Mt. Rushmore but much, much larger.) Today, the head and face of Crazy Horse have emerged from the mountain, but his body and the horse he will ride in the finished sculpture have yet to be completed. Private contributions and visitors' fees fund the project, which could take decades more to finish. Much of the work is being done by Ziolkowski's children.

The statue is but one aspect of the late Henry Standing Bear's effort to ensure Native American heritage is preserved and vibrant. Indian heritage museums, an educational framework that includes a Native American studies program at the University of South Dakota, and cultural activities such as the dance performance we saw are all part of the project. There, we also discovered that Chief Standing Bear had attended Carlisle Indian Industrial School as a child; this controversial school operated in the town where we live. The philosophy behind the Indian School is now much maligned. Its goal was to assimilate Native Americans at the expense of their indigenous traditions, with a mission to "kill the Indian" to "save the man." However, what he learned at the school became "a source of inspiration that Standing Bear would repeatedly draw upon to shape his enlightened understanding of cross-cultural relationships, as well as to find new ways of preserving his people's culture and history."[1] The dance we saw beneath the shadow of Crazy Horse provided a tangible expression of both the Lakota dancers' heritage and that of other indigenous tribes. Those moccasin-clad feet, stomping and chanting to the rhythm of native drums, articulated Standing Bear's vision—that we cannot forget their ancestors' history, which is so foundational to our nation.

Across the world in New Zealand, we became entranced by another native dance, this one performed by the fierce, tattooed Maori people

---

1 Crazy Horse Memorial. "Chief Henry Standing Bear–The Original Dreamer." Accessed November 10, 2021. https://crazyhorsememorial.org/story/the-history/chief-henry-standing-bear/.

of that island nation. Originating as a war dance, evolved versions of the *haka,* performed for tourists and at special occasions like weddings and funerals, still include vigorous, even menacing gestures, shouting, foot-stamping, and tongue thrusting. At my first haka, as I watched a large group of burly men and women with tattooed faces and bodies stomping toward me and shouting, the traditional dance certainly caught my attention. Once or twice, I had to remind myself that this was just a performance. When confronted by a group of Maori doing the haka on the battlefield, I can only imagine that many opponents would simply turn tail and run. My son, Josh, who spent a semester of college in New Zealand, played rugby there for fun and became a big fan of New Zealand's sports passion, the All-Blacks national rugby team. Before each game, the All-Blacks perform a haka on the field. Perhaps that helps explain New Zealand's many Rugby World Cup wins.

South Africa also has a successful rugby team, the Springboks. The way that Nelson Mandela used rugby to help a nation divided by apartheid find common ground is a compelling story. John Carlin's book, *Invictus: Nelson Mandela and the Game that Made a Nation,* and the subsequent movie, *Invictus,* starring Morgan Freeman and Matt Damon, dramatize that 1995 World Cup victory. In 2019, Mike and I saw a real-time demonstration of how South Africans, White and Black, still support the Springboks. By pure chance, we happened to be in the lobby of our airport hotel in Johannesburg when the Springboks landed from Japan and checked in after their World Cup victory against England. (New Zealand came in third that year.) The entire hotel, staff, and guests, went wild as the Springboks walked through, carrying the actual World Cup! A line formed on either side of the very large and fit victors as the enthusiastic audience cheered, clapped, and greeted the national heroes with spontaneous dancing and ululation that rang through the entire ground floor of the large hotel.

I smile when I remember a much quieter dance performance, a welcome dance and blessing ceremony, which a group of young girls performed in Laos. The shy group of preteens dressed in jewel-toned silks and elaborate gold headdresses executed the stylized steps and hand motions of several traditional dances with complete precision. At the end, they tied a white string around our wrists as a blessing. Wearing the string bracelet for three days is believed to ensure good fortune.

Another important way to engage in the culture of a place more fully is to explore and embrace the art. I love seeing the variety and sheer number of Buddha statues in the Southeast Asian countries we've visited. A definite art form as well as a religious symbol, these statues are carved in materials from marble to gilt to emerald to wood and differ among Buddhist sects and countries. We visited caves crammed full of tiny Buddhas, temples displaying life-size standing statues, and reclining Buddhas so large structures had to be built around them. Some of my favorites were the serene Buddhas, sitting in the Lotus Position, on the top terrace of the ancient temple of Borobudur. This UNESCO[2] site in Java dates to the eighth century. When the sun rose, the first rays of dawn set the worn volcanic stone statues afire with a steady glow so peaceful and mesmerizing that it made me believe—at least in the moment—that embracing the Buddha's teaching could, in fact, lead to enlightenment.

Museums are among the best places to see art, especially ancient artifacts and masterpieces in painting and sculpture. I studied a little art history in college. However, one doesn't need any formal art education to be awed by an El Greco in Madrid's Prada or a Turner in Washington's National Gallery of Art. The itineraries of package tours often include famous museums. We've appreciated those guided visits as a great way to rely on an expert to help us navigate the highlights of a large museum. But viewing paintings and other art cries out for a leisurely approach, so we've sometimes felt rushed by a tour's limited timeframe.

On our first visit to Paris, we arrived a few days early to have time to explore on our own. Then, we joined our riverboat cruise that included several more scheduled days in the city, including a half-day guided tour of the Louvre. Now, the Louvre is humongous. According to *CN Traveler*, it would take 200 days to see each of the 35,000 works of art on display at the museum; and that calculation only allows thirty seconds to view each piece.[3] So, having a guide to lead us to the best-known treasures of

---

2 United Nations Educational, Scientific, and Cultural Organization.
3 Betsey Blumenthal, "13 Things You Didn't Know about the Louvre." *CN Traveler*, May 18, 2020. https://www.cntraveler.com/story/things-you-didnt-know-about-the-louvre-museum.

the museum made a daunting task more manageable. Our charming and informative local guide had perfected a path through the Louvre that sampled famous sculptures like the Winged Victory of Samothrace and the Venus DeMilo; recognizable paintings like Delacroix's depiction of the bare-breasted female revolutionary in *Liberty Leading the People*; the Egyptian wing with its mummy, cartouches, and more. These works of art are spread among different sections of the building, so catching all the highlights involved considerable walking while breezing by tons of compelling art with no time to linger.

I must admit that I was psyched to see the Louvre's arguably most famous work of art, DaVinci's *Mona Lisa*. And I did get to see it, albeit, from the middle of a long, narrow room over the heads of a throng of tourists, all of whom seemed to be trying to take selfies with the iconic painting. And did I mention how tiny the *Mona Lisa* is? Less than two by three feet, something I didn't realize prior to glimpsing the original. Someday I'll go back to the Louvre and see more of the artworks at my own pace. Maybe even wend my way through the crowds and stand right in front of the *Mona Lisa*. (But no famous art selfies for me.)

On our next trip to Paris, Mike and I went to the Musée d'Orsay on our own and had a much better experience. I loved the Monets, and seeing the Van Goghs in person completely changed my previously tepid appreciation of his art. The brushwork and color of his paintings, like *Starry Night*, almost leaped off the wall with their vibrance and turned me into a fan.

We took a similar, self-guided approach to the wonderful Uffizi in Florence. Using the optional audio guide, we toured the museum at a leisurely tempo. I love the Uffizi, which is a boutique gallery compared to the massive Louvre. It houses many gems of art, from medieval triptychs gleaming with gilt to Botticelli's incandescent *Birth of Venus*.

Some of the best art I've found on our trips has not been housed in museums but tucked away in tiny towns, like the trompe d'oeil fresco on the wall of the cell phone store in a village in Provence or the baskets handwoven from local reeds by villagers in Botswana. Roadside stands from Uganda to Myanmar brim with wooden carvings, masks, and puppetry. I've found textiles I've loved in almost every place we've traveled—hand-dyed and -woven into intricate patterns from the wool of sheep, alpaca, or guanaco, as well as cotton and silk. And every region has its artists and artisans. We've bought lots of art geared toward the tourist market but also picked up paintings we've liked at random places along the way: a gallery in Taos; a street fair in St. Michaels, Maryland; a community exhibit in a hilltop village in France; a beachfront shop in St. Lucia.

And we always seek out workshops and other venues where we can see local artists at work. Outside Nairobi, Kenya, we visited a small cottage industry that created clay beads. We watched the workers, mostly women, use trays of various sizes to form the clay into balls of uniform diameter, paint the colorful designs, and fire the finished product in kilns. Although their ultimate product was jewelry, necklaces, and bracelets, I bought loose beads, which I keep in a wooden bowl in the living room. Whenever I look at them, I remember the room full of smiling women chatting among themselves as they performed the tedious and exacting job of turning clay into beads. Our guide told us that these women were happy to count themselves employed in a nation struggling with joblessness. They also produced beautiful beads that are sold all over the world.

Travel can be an adventure, and I thrive on the way it pushes me outside my comfort zone. But, to truly appreciate the journey, I believe we must slow our pace and open ourselves to the whole experience. The true goal of travel lies not in filling each travel day with scheduled motion, plowing through a destination with a checklist of monuments, shops, or animals to see. Approaching travel that way may complete a checklist but we may never really "see" the place we're visiting. I suggest that the better and more fulfilling approach lies in creating space in each journey for the unexpected. For absorbing each location by making time for watching, listening, and learning the culture through its music, dance, and art. When Mike and I have allowed that space in our trips, we've reaped lasting memories that will enrich us for our entire lives.

Acknowledgments

WHEN I sat down to write this book, I knew I didn't want to write a typical travelogue that chronicles specific trips. I didn't want to talk about the best sight to see in Kathmandu or the most unique dining spot in Amsterdam. Such books are a valuable resource for any trip, and I often rely on them when visiting new places. But I don't have the interest or expertise for writing travel guides. Instead, I decided to write a series of mini-essays on aspects of my travels. I believed this framework could best convey the joys and perils of a life elevated by periodic trips around the country and the world.

For a fiction writer, turning to the world of nonfiction, especially memoir-writing, was a giant leap into murky territory. I owe a huge debt of gratitude to several people and organizations who helped me navigate that leap during the writing process and those who laid the foundation with their lifetime support. I want to acknowledge their kind assistance.

First, I want to thank my husband, Mike Knowlton, for providing so many of his wonderful photographs for this book. In these photos of our journeys, he has captured the beauty of the places, people, and animals we've encountered in a way that goes well beyond the capability of my words. Mike, in my writing as in life, is my rock. He reads my early drafts, gives me sound advice, and copes gracefully with all the hours I spend writing.

Second, I want to thank my parents, Robert and Virginia Rothenberger, who instilled in me an early love of reading and fostered my continued addiction to the written word. Their nurturing provided me with a strong foundation for life, and—although not without some turmoil and reluctance—they supported my desire to explore new ideas and travel to unfamiliar places. I miss them every day.

I want to thank a host of people who have helped arrange my travels with Mike, family, and friends. Our Carlisle-based travel agent, Sandy Walker, has helped us design many trips, some off-the-shelf, some unique. I wish her happiness in her new journey into retirement. I also want to highlight Kim Guth's special role in introducing us to more and more of Africa with her expertise in designing the perfect safari. Many others have also helped us arrange great trips worldwide, and I appreciate their help.

I can't forget the many guides, riverboat/small ship/barge staff, and drivers who've helped us find joy in each new journey while ensuring that the excitement focuses on the new sights we've encountered rather than the logistics of the trip.

I'd also be remiss if I didn't thank those who've traveled with Mike and me on some of our adventures. As I outline in the book, good traveling companions can always enhance a journey. These fellow travelers include my brother, Rock Rothenberger; Steve and Betty Wing; Pete and Chris Gawron; Mike and Kathy Sehestedt; Sheryl Floyd; Craig Zwillinger; Jeff Gebhart; Connie and Terry Weiss; and the entire Knowlton family: Josh, Laura, Julia, Mia, Steve, Pam, Dave, Nancy, Coe, and Denny Kuehn.

I also want to thank the early review group who gave me feedback on this manuscript, moral support, and more. This group includes Joan West, Pat LaMarche, Phyllis Orenyo, Andrew Carey, and Val Muller.

I'm so grateful for the support of the entire crew at Sunbury Press, especially: Publisher Lawrence Knorr, who suggested that *Beyond the Sunset* be published in two volumes so there would be enough room for the photos and also designed an outstanding cover; Jennifer Cappello, whose superb editing helps enhance each new book I write, whether fiction or nonfiction; and Crystal Devine, who is adept at the technical aspect of production. And I can't forget my marketing team, Adrian Stouffer and Kim Lehman, who adapted gracefully to the challenge of promoting a nonfiction book

Finally, I want to thank all my readers. I hope that you, too, find a road to travel that suits your interests and lifestyle. Each of us may have different travel ambitions, whether they involve journeying to faraway places or just escaping into the written page. But whatever your path, I encourage you to dream big and step outside your comfort zone. Safe travels.

P.S.— Please leave a review of *Beyond the Sunset* on Amazon or Goodreads. And, of course, tell your friends about the book. Thank you.

About the Author

SHERRY KNOWLTON is the award-winning author of the Alexa Williams suspense novels, including *Dead of Autumn*, *Dead of Spring*, and *Dead on the Delta*. Her lifelong passion for books started as a child when she would sneak a flashlight to bed so she could read beneath the covers. All the local librarians knew her by name.

Now retired from executive positions in government and the health insurance industry, Sherry is "rewriting retirement" by turning her passion for writing into a new career. She draws on her professional background and worldwide travel experiences as inspiration for her writing.

Sherry and her husband, Mike, began their journey together in the days of peace and music when they traversed the country in a hippie van. Embracing the travel experience, they continue to explore far-flung places around the globe. These stories and more are recounted in her two-part travel memoir, *Beyond the Sunset*.

When she's not on the road, Sherry lives in the mountains of South-central Pennsylvania, where her Alexa Williams suspense series is set. Learn more at SherryKnowlton.com.

About the Photographers

'Elephant Adventure.' Mike and Sherry Knowlton at
Four Seasons Tented Camp Golden Triangle near
Chang Rai, Thailand. 2014

MIKE KNOWLTON has been traveling, camera in hand, since the early 1970s. Through his travels, he has discovered countless places of amazing beauty, come close to wild animals in their native habitats, and met people from cultures very different than his own. He firmly believes that if more people embraced learning about other countries and their cultures, whether in person or through other means, much of the divisiveness that exists in today's world could be bridged. Similarly, the conservation of endangered species would surely be enhanced if more people developed an appreciation for these animals in the wild.

Mike approaches his photography as photo journeys in which he strives to capture compelling images of the people, places, and animals he encounters. He wants each photograph to convey the perception of a unique experience or sense of place so that the viewer can share in his journeys.

Mike exhibits his photography primarily in Southcentral Pennsylvania, where he lives. However, his work hangs in private homes and other settings throughout the United States.

SHERRY KNOWLTON has been a photographer since she first used a brownie camera at age five. However, she has only begun to concentrate on photography as an art form in recent years. Much of her renewed interest in photography was spurred by her travels around the globe—and the compelling photo opportunities she encountered.

Sherry is particularly intrigued by serene landscapes, vertical lines, and patterns in nature/wildlife as well as the symbols and icons of societies. Instead of vast landscapes or majestic scenes, she prefers to focus on a perfect vignette or an interesting pattern within the broader panorama. She's fascinated by puppets, Buddha figures, and other secular and religious emblems that reflect the heart and soul of a culture. In her work, Sherry often explores images that blur the line between photography and painting. She exhibits her work regularly in various locations in Southcentral Pennsylvania.

CPSIA information can be obtained
at www.ICGtesting.com
Printed in the USA
BVHW091318180922
646972BV00002B/5